ECHOES OF THE WORD

Echoes of the Word

Leander E. Keck

CASCADE *Books* • Eugene, Oregon

ECHOES OF THE WORD

Copyright © 2015 Leander E. Keck. All rights reserved. Except for brief quotations in critical publications or reviews, no part of this book may be reproduced in any manner without prior written permission from the publisher. Write: Permissions. Wipf and Stock Publishers, 199 W. 8th Ave., Suite 3, Eugene, OR 97401.

Cascade Books
An Imprint of Wipf and Stock Publishers
199 W. 8th Ave., Suite 3
Eugene, OR 97401

www.wipfandstock.com

ISBN: 978-1-4982-0673-0

Cataloguing-in-Publication data:

Keck, Leander E.

 Echoes of the word / Leander E. Keck.

 x + 188 p. ; 23 cm.

 ISBN: 978-1-4982-0673-0

 1. Preaching. 2. Sermons, American. I. Title.

BS534.5 K42 2015

Manufactured in the U.S.A.

for Ann

Contents

Preface | ix

PART 1: *The Discipline of Hearing* | 1
1 Exegesis as a Theological Discipline | 3
2 Listening To and Listening For | 11

PART 2: *The Presence of the Prior Word* | 29
3 Challenged by the Greek Precedent | 31
4 Energized by Jewish Beginnings | 43
5 Paul: Problem and Promise | 53
6 Death and Afterlife in the New Testament | 67

PART 3: *The Word as Criterion* | 85
7 The Penetrating Word | 87
8 Scripture and Canon | 97
9 The Gospel's Promise of Salvation | 109

PART 4: *A Word for Bearers of the Word* | 121
10 Our Identity's Dimensions | 123
11 A Word for Us Theologians | 131
12 Is There Good News for Ministers Too? | 139
13 The Fear of the Lord Is the Beginning of Knowledge | 155

PART 5: *The Word Borne* | 161
14 Summoned to Christian Unity | 163
15 King Jesus? | 169
16 Are You the Coming One? | 175
17 Promise and Hope | 181

Preface

CONCERN FOR THE VIGOR of the Christian faith was an important factor in selecting the contents of this book: essays, addresses, and sermons given during the last decades of the previous century. The persistent question was, Is what was said in the past worth saying again, now to a new and wider audience? That question led to another: "Worth" for whom? It turned out that the readers envisioned now are probably like the hearers envisioned then.

None of these pieces was presented to audiences of mostly academics; they were given to hearers who were not specialists in biblical scholarship. Many audiences, however, included theological faculty and students, while pastors and lay folk constituted others. The sermons were addressed to various congregations.

These pieces are not a cross-section of my work; nor do they mount an argument or advocate a specific idea. The selection does, however, represent an important aspect of my vocation as a professor of New Testament: the commitment to teach also beyond the academic classroom. So the person who probably knows best whether these works from the past are worth publishing now is the reader who also ponders seriously the import of Christian faith in today's maelstrom. The stubborn endurance of the theological issues seething beneath manifest uncertainties and conflicts, then and now, gives these diverse pieces a measure of consistency; it also suggests the book's structure and title.

More important, if the word spoken then is worth reading now, it is because Scripture's capacity to unmask human foibles, as well as to promise an alternative, also persists. Gathered into these pages, then, are various attempts to say a perceptive, pertinent word into one circumstance after another during momentous decades (1959–1992) when occasionally one could also glimpse something new but ill-formed aborning. While

PREFACE

I owe the reader neither confession nor apology for what was said, and not said, a brief comment about the stance and tone of these selections is appropriate.

Running through these speeches and sermons are four convictions, usually left unstated. (1) As the church's canon, the Bible has a dual role: it not only funds Christian thought and morals, but it also judges their inadequate and distorting forms, however well-intended or "meaningful." (2) Since faith is not reducible to belief (or believing) because it is essentially trust (or trusting), what we trust most deeply expresses our real, operative religion. (3) That being the case, our culture, too, can be read as a religious text, depicting who we are because of what we trust; on the other hand, Scripture discloses what rightly trusting the Trustworthy One enables us to be and do. (4) Between hearing the Word in Scripture and re-saying it lies the task of understanding both texts theologically, for without such understanding—not to be confused with explanation—our own words readily become mere chatter.

So, then, as a teaching student of the New Testament, I sought to illumine and address current issues as a theological exegete, without repeating what was being said already (even if I often agreed with it), and also without simply being different by being "difficult." My contribution, if any, would be to say the often unsaid, the commonly neglected, the theologically disturbing, in order to address factors and forces beneath the surface symptoms (seldom explaining what I was trying to do). Instead of exposing other people's sins, I would try to elicit selfcriticism, remembering that the gospel repeatedly brought hope into our kind of world.

The manuscripts, written as scripts for the ear, have an oral style that is retained in pages meant to be read. The style is often lean (purged of unnecessary words) so that the hearer can follow the argument more easily, and generally free of the then current "in" words, lest using them impede serious thought. In retrospect, I doubt whether even impassioned delivery would have made it easier to comprehend the theologically dense passages. In any case, apart from minor editorial changes and occasional deletions, these texts remain as given. The occasions for which they were prepared, often important for understanding better what was said at the time, are noted in the Introductions to each cluster of speeches. That I would now say some things differently, or not at all, should need no explanation. These discourses are still what they attempted to be then—echoes of the Word.

PART 1

The Discipline of Hearing

Interpreters of enduring literature know that the art of hearing is more important than the skill of speaking. Those who interpret Scripture, Sunday after Sunday, know intuitively, as well as experientially, that the Word must be heard before it can be re-said. Fruitful hearing, though an art, is also a discipline that can be learned. Its name is exegesis.

The two addresses that together serve as the overture to the rest of the collection were given in quite different settings. The first sounded notes that later were repeated, amplified and, I trust, played in more nuanced tones. It was, in effect, my inaugural lecture at Vanderbilt Divinity School, given in September, 1959. (Years later I discovered that Union Theological Seminary in Richmond, Virginia, had published Professor James May's lecture on the Old Testament, under the same title!) In Nashville, among this newly appointed assistant professor's hearers were his new colleagues, his students from a part of the country wholly unknown to him, and, surprisingly, Vanderbilt's Chancellor, B. Harvie Branscomb, a distinguished New Testament scholar previously at Duke University. The lecture is published here for the first time.

The second piece is a slightly modified version of an address given thirteen years later at the Assembly of the Tennessee Association of Christian Churches (Disciples of Christ), meeting in Clarksville. The text was assigned: "You shall receive power" (Acts 1:8). The address was later outfitted with footnotes and published in *Interpretation* 27 (1973). Here it is paired with the inaugural lecture because it makes concrete what was said or implied in 1959 and in my 1978 book, *The Bible in the Pulpit*.

1

Exegesis as a Theological Discipline

At the beginning of our year's work, it is good to focus attention on that part of the theological enterprise which traditionally has been the foundation of the whole—exegesis. Not a few would hold that if the Christian faith is built on the apostles and prophets, the explication of it is built on the exegesis of the apostolic literature. But even if this were admitted, our task would only be stated, for generally speaking, we lack an adequate understanding of what exegesis involves and of how it is related to theology as a whole.

How, then, should we understand exegesis? The dictionary definition—that it is the critical interpretation of a text—is not adequate, because our problem is precisely that we are no longer confident that we know what interpretation involves. Likewise, the old adage that exegesis reads the text's meaning in but eisegesis reads it out is too simple because every exegetical effort combines ex- and eisegesis. No one approaches a text with complete neutrality.

Complete neutrality, however, was the ideal of an earlier time. Thus Heinrich August Wilhelm Meyer set himself such a goal in 1829, when he wrote the first volume of the now famous German commentary series that still bears his name. His Preface included the following remarks:

> The interpreter of Paul, having thoroughly deprived himself of his own self, should have put on the whole individuality of the Apostle. . . . He should not think with his own head, nor feel with his heart. . . . Because of the meaning which the New Testament has for the Christian church . . . the exegesis of the New Testament as such has no system at all and may not have one . . .

> insofar as he is an exegete he is neither orthodox nor heterodox, neither supernaturalist nor rationalist . . . he is neither pious nor godless, neither moral nor immoral . . . for he has only the obligation to search out what the author says so that he might give this over as a pure result to the . . . dogmatician. . . . The relation of the explicated meaning to the teaching of philosophy, how it agrees with the dogmas of the church . . . —this is of no concern to the exegete as such.

Before we smile at an attitude so naively confident, let us remember that in a sense Meyer was asserting a vital Reformation principle—the independence of Scripture vis-à-vis the church and its ordinary theology. Nor should we forget that orthodoxy usually claims that the Bible contains nothing that does not support it, and that the task of the exegete is to exhibit this agreement. We need only recall the recent call for a "Conservative Translation of the Bible" and the controversy over how Isa 7:14 should have been translated by the RSV in order to realize that the independence of historical-critical exegesis has not yet been granted by many parts of the Christian church. What Meyer required, and what every exegete expects, is honest listening to what the Bible actually says, and understanding why it says it that way. This is nothing less than what that often castigated exegete, Karl Barth, has also said: that we should take the Bible at least as seriously as we take ourselves.

In other words, scientific exegesis has the right, even the duty, to pursue the text's own meaning as carefully as possible, and to "let the chips fall where they may." Thus far, Meyer was right. In addition, today we remind ourselves that if biblical study is not carried forward with a rigorous quest for the intended meaning of the text, we shall have compromised the canonical criterion by which the church can gauge her faithfulness. The independence of the exegete is not to be confused with academic irresponsibility. In fact, it has been precisely through relentless, independent biblical study that the church has been summoned once again to come to grips with what the Bible has to say.

What Meyer did not see, however, was that one cannot recover the meaning of the text by an exegesis that is disinterested, that precisely the identification with Paul that he demanded is precluded when the exegete himself is excluded. How am I to think Paul's thoughts after him if I may not use my own head? If my self is not engaged? How is the interpreter to take the meaning from the text if he is forbidden to bring anything to it? Meyer did not see that two presuppositions controlled his demand:

one, that ultimate questions could be so thoroughly dismissed from the mind of the exegete that he is free to recapture an objective past; two, that such a past would itself be an adequate source for subsequent meaning. But just as there is no presuppositionless thinking, so there is no presuppositionless exegesis. It is precisely this disturbing fact which makes our problem acute: what IS exegesis and how is it related to theology as such? If we can no longer think that an exegesis wholly free of presuppositions is either possible or desirable, are there any alternatives?

II

Looking briefly at several possibilities can help us move forward. The first was developed by the left wing of biblical criticism, on the assumption that scientific exegesis must carry on a continual war with the church and its interpretation. This can be seen clearly in what Albert Schweitzer taught us to call the Quest for the Historical Jesus. As the critical study of the Gospels advanced, not only did traditionalists defend these texts as completely reliable records of the life of Jesus, but some radicals completely rewrote the story of Jesus' life, and a few claimed that he had never existed at all. What began as a creative reinterpretation of the Gospels by David Friedrich Strauss ended in a hodge-podge of data and innuendo published in the early years of this century by Arthur Drews in Germany and by William B. Smith, a mathematician at Tulane University. In all such works, there is the constant theme that scientific historical exegesis is inevitably pitted against the church's theological tradition.

A second alternative was offered by what is known as historicism and it is associated with Adolf Harnack, the eminent church historian at Berlin. Though he too was critical of traditional dogma, he tried to serve the church by recalling it to what he believed was the original gospel of Jesus. In his epoch-making lectures, translated as *What is Christianity?* Harnack said, "The Christian religion is something simple and sublime—it means one thing and one thing only: eternal life in the midst of time, by the strength and under the eyes of God." Harnack believed that the eternally valid gospel addressed the essentially unchanging man in changing circumstances. As a historian, he knew very well that the gospel too had become many things. How, then, did he determine which part of the gospel's many changing expressions is eternally valid, and which part can be dismissed as expressing the historical circumstance in which it had been expressed, or as he put it, How does one separate the kernel from the husk? Harnack found the answer in history itself, as disclosed by historical research. "What was kernel here and what was husk, history has itself showed with unmistakable plainness, and by the shortest possible process. Husk was the whole of the Jewish limitations attaching to Jesus' message. . . ." Thus Harnack peeled away the historical context of Jesus' teaching to lay bare an eternally valid core which Paul's mission to Gentiles transformed into a universal religion, which was again and again transformed. For Harnack, the exegetical task was to recapture the gospel's original expression so that it could be the norm for later expressions. Thus historical research could disclose the true and living center of the Christian religion. Within this everchanging, culturally conditioned Christianity there exists a constant element to which we can respond in faith—the kernel disclosed by history.

After the Great War showed what history could be, it is little wonder that the third alternative was a violent reaction to Harnack's view. Thus in Barth's 1919 commentary on Romans, the meaning-giving center of the Bible was not found through historical research, and thus dependent on man, but was the wholly free, unexpected Word of God in the Bible's words. Not the kernel in the husk, but the direct, inbreaking Word of God which comes to man not as a datum to be analyzed but as a summons to be obeyed, precisely because it is a Word, which dissolves all notions about the search for a kernel because it is a Word from God. This, for Barth, is what the Bible attests and makes possible. The task of the exegete, then, is to press through the words of the text to the Word of God. All historical-critical work is at best only preliminary to listening for the Word in the words. Consequently, exegesis is theology and theology is exegesis. The dogmatician is nothing less than a systematic interpreter of Scripture.

How different from Meyer, who insisted that theology not contaminate exegesis! Yet, there is also a striking similarity between them. Meyer set out to exclude himself so he could think Paul's thoughts. Barth, in his Preface to the second edition of his Romans commentary, claims access to Paul by just the opposite means. It is not by excluding his own interests but by a relentless pressing of the issues that he claims at last to have come to grips with the issues with which Paul grappled, and thus also to have eliminated the assumed difference that twenty centuries create between Paul and modern man. Not by disinterested analysis does one understand and interpret Paul, but by becoming existentially invnolved in the crisis of man before God. Only then does one lay hold of the Word in the words, and so become able to write a commentary with Paul and not merely on him. The identification with Paul that Meyer demanded is achieved by Barth because he rejected Meyer's method. So also what Harnack sought—the confrontation of man as man with the eternal gospel—is unexpectedly reached by Barth who rejected Harnack's method with equal vigor.

Some of those who looked for a fourth alternative found Rudolf Bultmann to be the New Moses who could lead us to the Promised Land. Bultmann has the distinct advantage of being both a master of the historical-critical method and of working consciously with a theological perspective. For Bultmann, there is only one exegetical method—the historical-critical one. More radically than most of his peers, he applies it rigorously to the New Testament. But instead of excluding his own theology, as Meyer required, he pursues historical criticism until he lays hold of the understanding of human existence implied in the text. Like Barth, Bultmann assumes at the outset that the New Testament is the unique bearer of God's Word, and thus he refuses to treat it simply as a repository of early Christian ideas. But unlike Barth, Bultmann is not impatient to get the critical research done so that the real issues can be dealt with.

Interestingly, however, it is because Bultmann wants to take seriously both the historical-critical method and its results that he is under attack from theologians and exegetes alike. For as a result of his critical work, Bultmann has become aware that the New Testament presupposes an understanding of the world, of man, and of God that is so alien to ours that a real perception of the New Testament's message is impossible. At the same time, because he sees the New Testament as the bearer of the Word and not simply as the husk around a kernel of truth, he must take it seriously. But how can one take seriously the Word in the words if the words are rooted in essentially alien presuppositions? His solution is to recast the New Testament's understanding into terms that enable modern man to really hear and hearken to the Word of God and not merely listen to the strange words of the text. Thus without looking for timeless truths, Bultmann seeks to restate the New Testament in language that modern man may truly hear what it actually has to say.

Let me summarize what I have outlined as four alternative positions: first, attacking the church and its theology requires moderns to choose between exegesis and (true) theology; second, using the Scripture as source in the historical-critical quest for the permanently valid kernel in religion's ever-changing husk; third, identifying the brunt of the Bible with the Word of God which does not come as the result of historical work; and fourth, pursuing historical questions until the historicity of man is disclosed and restated in existential terms. Each of these has an element of truth which dare not be ignored. Yet each is vulnerable as well.

III

Let me suggest a different relationship between exegesis and theology. What I have in mind is rather simple: exegesis and theology are related in a continual dialogue. That is, the exegesis of Scripture is achieved when fundamental questions are raised and dealt with theologically. Where this lively conversation occurs, exegesis will provoke serious dialogue between the ancient text and the modern believer, essential for both exegesis and creative Christian faith. For exegesis places a question mark behind our theology, and our theological understanding assumes the validity of what exegesis discloses.

An example will take us to the heart of the matter. One basic datum for understanding Jesus' conception of his work is recorded in Lk 11:20: "If it is by the finger of God that I cast out demons, then the kingdom of God is come upon you." Critical exegesis not only attests the reliability of this logion but also connects the exorcising work to the preaching work of Jesus. Both the word and the deed are forms of announcing the kingdom. Exegesis can pursue the matter farther by relating the various relevant Gospel materials concerning the kingdom of God and Jesus' relation to it. To some extent it can also assist an historical reconstruction of the main features of Jesus' ministry with varying degrees of probability. The exegete can also discern the ways the Evangelists understood his mission. But here the exegete approaches the frontier of the discipline. That is, demonstrating that Jesus believed he was the herald and bearer of the kingdom raises the real question, Was he? Was Jesus what historical research indicates he believed himself to be? Did his career have the religious significance he apparently saw in it? And if not, if the kingdom did not come as he expected, was his own eschatology crucified with him? If so, did his resurrection transform it as it transformed him?

Such questions—the real religious questions—cannot be answered by doing more exegesis of more passages, because this process would either refine the questions or merely give us the answers of the early

EXEGESIS AS A THEOLOGICAL DISCIPLINE

Christians. The bankruptcy of such an approach is painfully manifest when we hear fellow believers try to answer theological questions by quoting texts that also need exegesis. Our substantive questions, raised by exegesis, are to be answered instead by decision, by obedient response to the Word heard in the words. When this begins to occur, the answer to our question will be found beyond exegesis, for it will have moved from the critical explanation of the text to wrestling with its claim to religious truth. In short, exegesis fulfills its function by raising the questions so that the Word might occur to us.

It will perhaps be objected that since the Bible contains the answers to man's questions; how can one say that the goal of exegesis is discovering the questions? This objection would be cogent if the Bible were a compendium of true ideas. Indeed, a popular notion about the Bible is not far from such a view. But even if that were the proper way of viewing the Bible, the real issue would be exactly the same: Can I believe that this humble and humiliated Jesus is the Christ whom God raised from the dead without responding to this claim as a Word about God from God?

Driven by the consequences of our exegesis to the frontier not only of our discipline but also by the nature of faith itself, we can become receptive to the Word. It is precisely when we become aware of the limits of our understanding that we face the deeper questions of faith. It is then that God can communicate that Word that can save us and make us free. There is no guarantee, of course, that this will occur because exegesis is not a procedure for producing the Word. If, however, we have been led to this possible event by following the narrow path of exegetical work, we can come to know in what sense the Bible becomes God's Word to us and for us. In addition, because the exegetes are members of the same community that produced and preserved the texts in the first place, they are willing to listen for the Word lest in our time they miss hearing what their forebears heard in theirs. Moreover, it is this same event of hearing the Word that draws us back to the text where we may now find that also its answers become ours, enabling us to share its witness. So our exegesis casts a double light: on the one hand, it illumines the text before us; on the other, it throws light on the interpreter as well.

One more question must be asked: How does this differ from Harnack's dialogue between exegesis and Christian history? He also wanted to determine the truth by a continual dialogue between the results of historical-critical exegesis and the subsequent manifestations of the Christian religion. The difference lies in this: whereas Harnack carried on his dialogue in the quest for the eternally valid core of religion, we enter it in the quest of that Word that can free us for our particular time and place, believing that the Word comes to us not in disembodied purity but in the warp and woof of our humanity and historicity, for thus did the Word once become flesh and blood among us.

If what has been said has any validity at all, our studies will summon us to a significant dialogue not only among the various disciplines in the curriculum but also within each of us. We may secretly try to emulate Jonah, to whom the Word of the Lord came as he sat in the shade of the cucumber vine, but our more likely model is the legendary Jacob who heard God's Word after he wrestled.

2

Listening To and Listening For
(Acts 1:8)

For the preacher, the art of hearing is more important than the art of speaking. This is especially true for "expository preaching," for unless the Word is heard it cannot be re-said. The text is the listening post where the preacher expects to hear a word for the situation in which he and his people find themselves. Perceptive hearing usually begins with *listening for*, with an attentiveness marked by expectation focused by one's situation. When the text and the situation are present to one another, one can begin to hear what the text means.

"Listening for" requires *listening to*; that is, a measure of exegetical skill. Exegesis, as I understand it, is not merely the enterprise of compiling learned notes that explain peculiarities of the wording, nor is it reducible to the effort to document the genealogy of ideas found in the text, though it usually includes both. Exegesis, rather, is the discipline of discerning as precisely as possible the subject matter of the text in its concreteness and of stating it in such a way that another can grasp it. The subject matter must be rethought so that the particular way in which a given text treats it can be expressed. It is especially important not to obscure the particularity of diverse writings into a "biblical point of view" which the authors might not have acknowledged. Historical-critical exegesis should facilitate perceptive hearing.

This essay shows how one student moved from analysis and exegesis to a sermon. In this case, the text was assigned: "You shall receive power" (Acts 1:8); the occasion was the annual Assembly of the Tennessee Association of Christian Churches (Disciples of Christ), which met in

PART 1: THE DISCIPLINE OF HEARING

Clarksville, Tennessee, in May, 1972. The article is devoted, accordingly, to a brief exegetical discussion of the text, followed by some reflections on the which represent an attempt to hear the force of the text in today's situation; thereafter comes the sermon itself, somewhat abbreviated.

Just as not every listening is a hearing, so exegesis, however knowledgeable, does not inevitably produce a discerned word. Often its immediate result is negative, disabusing us in matters great and small. We should not underestimate this negative result, for learning what the writer did not say can be as important as identifying what he did say. Minimally, exegesis should help us distinguish the voice of the text from our own echo. This distancing of the text from ourselves is necessary if it is to be free; only then can it intersect the present.

The intersecting must occur first within the exegete-preacher. The text in its integrity and the preacher in his, "warts and all," must be present to each other. Only then can he truly hear. Moreover, he ought to hear not only for himself but also for his congregation.

If he identifies with the congregation so that when the text meets him it accosts them as well, he exercises his priestly office. By claiming his own struggle to appropriate the burden of the text, he helps them claim theirs. On the other hand, if there is no struggle with the text, no exposure to it, the text will degenerate into a useful tool with which the preacher hopes to sanctify ideas he already has; worse still, the vitality of the text will suffocate under the assumption that "of course" he agrees with it, but that the congregation does not. Where the preacher does not align himself with the congregation so that he may articulate their common hearing/resistance, he aligns himself with the text against the congregation. But the hearers quickly perceive whether the preacher is with them in the hearing of the Word or whether, by siding with the text, he facilely insulates himself from hearing in order to use the text as he sees fit. Where there is authentic hearing, the preacher risks being vulnerable; where he is secure with the text, he does not need to hear for he already knows what he will do with it.

An Effort to Listen To

The opening section of Acts bristles with problems, most of which we can bypass here. Our text (1:8) is part of the farewell scene of 1:6–11; this consists of three elements: the exchange between the risen Jesus and his followers (vs. 6–8), the ascension (v. 9), and the word of the two (angelic) men in white robes (vs. 10–11). Structurally, the ascension is the central item, but materially it is not the most important, for the accent falls on the words which frame it. On both sides we find words of promise: that of the angelic figures concerns the evidently distant future (the parousia), while that of the risen Jesus concerns what is imminent (the coming of the Spirit). Evidently the word of Jesus holds good until the word of the angelic figures comes true. That is, the word of Jesus is valid for the remainder of history.

The forty-day period unites the Spirit-impelled time of the apostles. But also this transition time is under the aegis of the Spirit-assuming that the Revised Standard Version (and the New English Bible) translates correctly: "after he had given commandment through the Holy Spirit to the apostles whom he had chosen" rather than "had chosen through the Holy Spirit."[1] The beginning of the church's story is generally analogous to the beginning of the story of Jesus: In both cases, the narrative proper begins with a sermon linked with the arrival of the Spirit (Luke 4; Acts 2); in both, the period immediately preceding is not totally devoid of the Spirit (Luke 1–2; Acts 1); in both, what is promised is contrasted with John the Baptist (Luke 3:16; Acts 1:5ff.). Evidently, Luke[2] regards the story of the church as the continuation of the story of Jesus, and he sees both as two phases of the same kind of story—one set in motion by the Spirit.[3]

Luke has no interest in what Jesus taught about the Kingdom (v. 3);[4] what concerns him is the command not to leave Jerusalem until "the Father's promise" has been fulfilled, a promise relayed previously (v. 4; cf. also Luke 24:49. We must by-pass here the whole question of Jerusalem vs. Galilee appearances). To our surprise, the promise is a variant of what

---

1. So Ernst Haenchen, *The Acts of the Apostles: A Commentary*, trans. B. Noble, et al. (Philadelphia: Westminster, 1971), *ad loc.*; J. Munck thinks "through the Holy Spirit" goes with both the choosing and the instructing. *The Acts of the Apostles* (Anchor Bible), *ad loc.*

2. Calling the author "Luke" does not commit one to identifying the writer.

3. Given the clear importance of the Spirit for Luke's whole perspective on the narrative, it is odd that J. H. E. Hull is disquieted (his term) by the fact that Jesus said so little about the Spirit, that he promised it only near the end (in the Fourth Gospel) and after the resurrection (Luke–Acts). Hull, *The Holy Spirit in the Acts of the Apostles* (London: Lutterworth, 1967), chap. 1.

4. I do not see why R. F. Zehnle concludes that the apostles did not grasp the full meaning of Jesus' postresurrection teaching "about the universal nature of the kingdom" when no content is reported. Zehnle, *Peter's Pentecost Discourse*, SBL Monograph Series 15 (Nashville: Abingdon, 1971), 104.

PART 1: THE DISCIPLINE OF HEARING

Luke 3: 16 gives as a word of the Baptist: "I baptize you with water; but he who is mightier than I is coming, . . . he will baptize you with the Holy Spirit and with fire." This saying appears in different forms in all the Gospels.[5] In Acts 11:16, however, Luke has Peter quote the form found in Acts 1:5 (with slight changes in word order).

Acts 1:5 (and 11:16) appears to contrast water baptism with Spirit baptism. Yet the subsequent narrative assumes that they belong together: Peter baptizes with water because the Spirit has already come on Cornelius (10:47), and Paul rebaptizes those who know only John's baptism so that the disciples at Ephesus can receive the Spirit as well (19:1–7). Evidently, Luke is not interested in a contrast between water and Spirit per se, but in highlighting the distinctive thing which Christian baptism brought—the Spirit. Accordingly, in reporting Jesus' baptism, Luke did not say explictly that John baptized him, since that might suggest that John's baptism did convey the Spirit. The Spirit is intimately associated with Jesus and the church, not with John.[6] Moreover, though according to Luke 3:16 John promised that the stronger one would baptize with Holy Spirit and fire, Luke never has Jesus himself impart the Spirit, as does the Fourth Gospel (John 20: 22).[7] In Acts 1:5, Jesus appears to correct John's promise: now it is the Father's promise that is about to be fulfilled.

---

5. Matt 3:11—"I baptize you with water for repentence but he who is coming after me is mightier than I, . . . ; he will baptize you with the Holy Spirit and with fire" (followed by harvest metaphor).

Mark 1:7–8—"After me comes he who is mightier than I, ... I have baptized you with water; but he will baptize you with the Holy Spirit" (no harvest metaphor).

John 1:26—"I baptize with water; but among you stands one whom you do not know..."

John 1:33—"he who sent me to baptize with water said to me, 'He on whom you see the Spirit descend and remain, this is he who baptizes with the Holy Spirit.'"

6. There is a tension between Luke's own perspective and the angelic promise to Zechariah that John would be filled with the Spirit (Luke 1:15). Yet, only Jesus' birth, not John's, is traced to the work of the Spirit. Elizabeth and Zechariah are "filled with the Spirit" (Luke 1:41, 67), but only as the basis of their prophetic announcements. Luke 1:80 refrains from using "the Holy Spirit" (Luke's characteristic phrase) and merely says that John "grew strong in spirit." Thus Luke reserves the Spirit for Jesus and the church. W. Barnes Tatum, however, reasons differently. He regards Luke 1:15 as expressing also Luke's own view: John is endowed with the spirit of prophecy, as are Elizabeth and Zechariah, and this links John with the Epoch of Israel (following Conzelmann) and distances him from Jesus. "The Epoch of Israel: Luke 1–11 and the Theological Plan of Luke–Acts," *NTS* 13 (1966/67) 184ff.

7. I fail to see how G. W. H. Lampe, in an otherwise useful survey, can cite John 20:22 to illustrate that "certain passages from the Fourth Gospel serve to make explicit"

Implicit in what Acts shows is what the Fourth Gospel says—that the Spirit comes to the church only after Jesus departs (John I 6:7), though Luke does not say that the Father will send him in response to Jesus' request (John 15: 16), or in Jesus' name (John 14:26), much less that Jesus himself will come (John 14:18). But Luke agrees with John in saying that the exalted Jesus will send the Spirit (Acts 2:33; John 15:26). However, whereas in the Fourth Gospel the coming of the Spirit to Jesus is important only for the Baptist (John 1:19-34), in Luke it is decisive for Jesus and his mission (note how the Spirit links the materials in Luke 3:1-23; 4:1-30). What was first given to Jesus is later given to the church; what unites Luke's two-volume story is the work of the Spirit.

How Luke understands the Spirit in the time of the church begins to emerge in our pericope. In Acts 1:6, Jesus' followers ask whether at this time he will restore the Kingdom to Israel, a reference to the hope expressed in Luke 24:21.[8] Jesus' reply consists of three elements: a critical response to the question, a promise, and a commission. The structure of the reply indicates that the promise and the commission together constitute the alternative to the question asked. The apostles are not to understand themselves on the verge of a restored kingdom but on the verge of power and mission.[9]

Clearly vv. 6-8 interpret v. 5, the promised baptism of the Holy Spirit. It is not necessary to conclude that the apostles asked about the restoration[10] of the Kingdom because they inferred that this would follow

---

what is implied in Acts. "The Holy Spirit in the Writings of St. Luke," in *Studies in the Gospels: Studies in Memory of R. H. Lightfoot*, edited by D. E. Nineham (Oxford: Blackwell, 1966), 200.

8. Acts 3:21 indicates that the national hope has not been annulled. Perhaps one can also appeal to 23:6 where "the hope" is linked with "the resurrection of the dead." Haenchen regards this as an allusion to the Messianic hope, while Conzelmann does not because he sees the whole phrase as a hendiadys.

9. The extent to which we ought to see here an allusion to the problem of the delay of the parousia is debated. We must bypass this problem completely here.

10. Acts 1:6 uses the verb *apokathistanein* (RSV: "restore") and 3:21 has the noun *apokatastasis*, which the RSV renders "establishing," thereby obscuring the terminological continuity. In 3:21 the risen Jesus is said to have been taken to heaven until the time of restoration of everything which God promised through the prophets. This evidently alludes, in part at least, to the national hope. Acts 15:16-17 (drawing on Jer 12:15 and Amos 9:11-12) also should be considered, for it speaks of rebuilding the ruins of the dwelling of David. That the election of Mathias belongs with the restoration theme has been suggested by J. Schmitt, "L'église de Jerusalem ou la 'restauration' d'Israel d'apres les cinq chapitres des livre des Acts," *RSR* 27 (1953) 209ff. Interestingly,

PART 1: THE DISCIPLINE OF HEARING

from the arrival of the eschatological Spirit.[11] The text is not interested in exposing the flow of ideas in the apostles' minds. Nor is it necessary to regard their question as a mere foil for Jesus' answer (so Conzelmann and Haenchen). Rather, Luke appears to acknowledge that the hope for Israel, which the apostles shared, was not cancelled; the point at issue is the time (indicated also by the word order).[12] This has been set by the Father; Luke suggests that Jesus knows this time (Luke omitted Mark 13:32, according to which the Son does not know). But by refusing to disclose or discuss it, Luke has Jesus implicitly set aside a discussion of the restoration itself. Luke's interest is in interpreting the baptism of the Holy Spirit. For him, the Holy Spirit means power which manifests itself in diverse ways throughout the following narrative: glossolalia (Acts 2:4; 10:44–46; 19:6), healing power (6:8, and other stories where it is assumed), guidance (13:1–3; 16:6; 19:21), and especially power for articulate witness.

In the New Testament, witness terminology is concentrated in Luke–Acts and in John. Interestingly, John never uses the nouns *martys* or *martyrion*, but perfers the verb *martyrein*; on the other hand, these nouns appear most frequently in Acts.[13] This datum alerts us not to confuse Lukan with Johannine usage. The distinguishing accent in Johannine use is the concentration of witness on the person of Jesus;[14] it concerns

---

Luke omitted Mark 9:13, according to which Elijah is to come and restore all things (using the same verb).

11. Such an interpretation would commend itself had Jesus spoken of the outpouring of the Spirit, as does Peter in 2: 17–18 (using Joel). In that case, the apostles could have inferred national restoration because it was one of the End-time events. But is there sufficient evidence that the eschatological giving of the Spirit was spoken of as a baptism? That Luke associates these expressions is clear; that the apostles would have done so is not. The interpretation questioned here was advanced by Franz Mussner, "Die Idee der Apokatastasis in die Apostelgeschichte," in *Lex Tua Veritas: Festschrift für Hubert Junker zur Vollendung des siebzigsten Lebensjahres am 8. August 1961, dargeboten von Kollegen, Freunden und Schülern*, edited by H. Gross and F. Mussner (Trier: Paulinus, 1961), 296.

12. Also Mussner (ibid.) sees this, pointing out that were Jesus to repudiate the restoration, he would be contradicted by Peter in 3:21. Mussner also suggests that Isa 49:6 is in the background here.

13. For a general discussion, see H. Strathmann's article on *martyrein*, et al., in Gerhard Kittel, ed., *TDNT* 4 (Grand Rapids: Eerdmans, 1967).

14. Note how John 5:31–40 emphasizes testifying "concerning me": the witness is borne by John the Baptist, by Jesus' works, by the Father, and by the Scriptures, respectively. For a discerning discussion of the witness theme in John, see Josef Blank, *Krisis* (Freiburg: Lambertus, 1964), 198–225.

his identity[15] and authorization.[16] Moreover, Jesus himself is a witness on earth to what he has seen and heard with the Father (John 3:32); later the Spirit shall also witness to Jesus (John 15:26),[17] as will the disciples (John 15:27). Presumably their testifying also centers in the person of Jesus and his salvific work. Moreover, John's avoiding the noun "witness" suggests that he is not interested in the apostles as definitive witnesses but only in witnessing activity. Accordingly, 1 John 5:9–12 implies that everyone who believes in the Son is to witness because he has within himself God's own witness to the Son, namely (eternal) life. While the Johannine understanding of witnessing doubtless includes attesting the actuality of the event of Jesus (as 1 John 1:1ff. emphasizes: cf. also John 21:24), this is the primary accent for Luke.

In Acts, Luke insists that the apostles are witnesses because they are eyewitnesses to the history of Jesus.[18] This note is struck also at the end of his Gospel (Luke 24:48), where the risen Jesus summarizes central themes of the kerygma and says, "You are witnesses of these things" — that is, you are eyewitnesses and therefore can bear witness to their factuality and import. The same theme appears also at the beginning of the Gospel (Luke 1:1–4), where Luke says that what he is about to narrate is traceable to eyewitnesses (*autoptai*).[19] When the circle of the Twelve is

---

15. John the Baptist witnesses that Jesus is the Son of God (1:34), and implies that he preexisted as well (1:15).

16. Jesus' deeds witness that the Father sent him (5:36).

17. In John, the Spirit (Paraclete) also bean witness in a forensic sense: He will convict the world with regard to sin, righteousness, and judgment (16:7–11). Unfortunately, the RSV obscures this point by rendering *elegxei* as "convince" rather than "convict." That the Johannine understanding of witness has a forensic aspect also with regard to Jesus' self-witness in the hostile world has been seen by Blank, *Krisis*, 198.

18. That the witness theme is not part of the kerygmatic traditions but Luke's own emphasis has been argued persuasively. See Ulrich Wilckens, *Die Missionsreden der Apostelgeschichte* (Neukirchen-Vluyn: Neukirchener, 1962–63), pp. 145ff.; Charles Talbert, *Luke and tha Gnostics* (Nashville: Abingdon, 1966), 23; A. J. B. Higgins, "The Preface to Luke and Kerygma in Acts," in *Apostolic History and the Gospel: Biblical and Historical Essays Presented to F. F. Bruce on His 60th Birthday*, edited by W. W. Gasque and R. P. Martin (Grand Rapids: Eerdmans, 1970), 85.

19. The debated question of the extent to which the preface to Luke has in view also the content of Acts is discussed recently by Higgins, who concludes that "Acts is an essential part of the confirmation Luke is able to provide, because so much of it, and not only the preaching of the church leaders, is a witnessing to the truth of the historia Jesu which Theophilus had learned . . ." Higgins, "The Preface," 82–83. That the Lukan preface pertains to Acts also is asserted by Günter Klein as well. "Lukas 1, 1–4 als theologisches Program," in *Rekonstruktion und Interpretation* (Munich: Kaiser,

reconstituted after the ascension, Luke has Peter insist that Judas' successor must be chosen from those "who have accompanied us during all the time that the Lord Jesus went in and out among us, beginning from the baptism of John until the day when he was taken up from us . . ." (1:21–22). In short, the apostolic circle is drawn only from those who can give a reliable account of the entire public Jesus-event. Charles Talbert has pointed out that Luke so writes his Gospel that everything which is reported was seen by Galileans (including the burial, Luke 23:55).[20] Moreover, during the forty days with Jesus they heard him teach and ate with him.[21] Luke's intent is clear: Everything in the story of Jesus which the apostles are about to announce to the world they have seen with their own eyes. Accordingly, except for Acts 14:14 Paul is not called an apostle, for his authorization is not that of an eyewitness; nonetheless, Luke has even Paul make precisely the same point: "for many days he appeared to those who came up with him from Galilee to Jerusalem, who are now his witnesses to the people" (Acts 13:31).[22] That Paul himself would have spoken of Jesus' resurrection appearances without including himself among the recipients is precluded by 1 Corinthians 15. Yet it is

---

1969), 260. Klein also implies that Luke 1:2 should not be rendered "who from the beginning were eyewitnesses and ministers of the word" but "who from the beginning were eyewitnesses and became ministers of the word" (248–49).

20. Talbert summarizes aptly: "The witness motif is one that dominates both Lukan volumes. Galilee is the scene of the gathering of the witnesses and of the public teaching which the chosen ones hear and understand. There is no time from the beginning of Jesus' ministry in Galilee to the point of his ascension . . . that he is without the Galileans . . . They are witnesses to all these things. If Acts records the testimony borne by the witnesses, Luke is the record of their preparation to bear witness." *Luke and the Gnostics*, 27.

21. The probable meaning of *synalizomenos* in Acts 11:4, as confirmed by 10: 41, where Peter speaks of witnesses "who ate and drank with him after he rose from the dead."

22. I cannot agree with I. Howard Marshall's claim that "Luke . . . in reality is close to Paul in his concept of apostleship and witness," and that Luke's requirement that the apostles be eyewitnesses of Jesus' ministry has been overemphasized by those who distinguish the Lukan from the Pauline view. Such harmonizing impedes understanding. "The Resurrection in the Acts of the Apostles," *Apostolic History and the Gospel*, 106-7. The distinctively Lukan understanding of The Twelve and of apostleship has been explored by Günter Klein, *Die zwölf Apostle*, FRLANT 77 (Göttingen: Vandenhoeck & Ruprecht, 1961). Herbert Braun pointed out that for Paul, witness terminology never has Jesus' resurrection as its content. "Zur Terminologie der Acta von der Auferstehung Jesus," in *Gesammelte Studien zum Neuen Testament und seiner Umwelt* (Tübingen: Mohr Siebeck, 1962), 174 n.35.

important for Luke that Paul, whom he portrays as specially chosen to be a witness to Jesus,[23] appropriate and transmit the unanimous testimony of the original eyewitnesses. In this way, the gospel in Paul's churches is as securely founded as it is in Palestine.

While the apostolic witness includes various motifs,[24] the focal point is Jesus' passion and resurrection. Talbert has observed that nowhere else in his Gospel did Luke take such care to point out that the incidents which constitute this narrative were witnessed, that is, seen.[25] In this way he could show that the apostles were truthful when they repeatedly emphasized that they were witnesses to the death and resurrection (Acts 1:22; 2:32; 3:15; 4:33; 5:32; 10:41). Strictly speaking, Luke did not say that the apostles witnessed (saw) the resurrection. Nowhere in the New Testament does anyone see this event; for such a report one must go to the apocryphal Gospel of Peter. What Luke actually reports is that the apostles saw, and ate with, the Jesus who had been killed and buried; they asserted the resurrectedness of Jesus because he showed himself to them with "proofs" (Acts 1:3 apparently generalizes the sort of incident reported in Luke 24:36-43).

Actually, Luke is concerned to guarantee the whole Jesus tradition. Günter Klein properly infers that, from Luke's point of view, what Theophilus had been taught could not be guaranteed adequately by his predecessors (Luke 1:1-4, among these we now place Mark and Q!), and that Luke assumed that his own work could do so.[26] Whether Gnosticism was the dominant danger which Luke had in view, as Talbert argued, or whether this was but one of several factors need not be decided here. What we do need to see is Luke's pervasive concern to legitimate

---

23. In Acts 22:15, Ananias is reported as having said to Paul, "you will be a witness for him to all men of what you have seen and heard." In 26:15-16 Paul reports that Jesus himself had said, "I have appeared to you for this purpose, to appoint you to serve and bear witness to the things in which you have seen me and to those in which I will appear to you..."

24. Acts 2:37-40 (repentence and the promise of the Spirit); 3:11-16 (healing in Jesus' name, repentence, ascension, parousia, judgment); 5:27-32 (exaltation, repentance, forgiveness); 10:34-43 (sketch of Jesus' ministry, post-Easter associations, command to preach, Jesus the destined Judge, forgiveness in his name witnessed by OT); 13:16-41 (Jesus' innocence, fulfillment of Scripture, forgiveness, freedom from the law, warning); 20:21 (no reference to resurrection because the speech is given to believers; repentance and faith); 28:33 (no reference to resurrection, Kingdom of God, fulfillment of Scripture).

25. *Luke and the Gnostics*, 30.

26. "Lukas 1,1-4 als theologisches Programm," 258.

the gospel by showing that it rests on eyewitness reports. Accordingly, the apostolic kerygrna in Acts can contain thumbnail sketches of the ministry of Jesus (Acts 2:22-36; 10:36-43; 13:23-41) but cannot use the birth stories,[27] or Jesus' postresurrection work. That the Lord has been taken to heaven can be asserted because this was seen; what he is doing there, other than sitting at the right hand (except for one instance when Stephen sees him standing, 7:56), is left unsaid, apart from momentary appearances as in Paul's case. In other words, it is possible that Luke uses "primitive" Christian theological traditions because this relatively undeveloped material was congenial to the witness theme, which called for concentration on those things which could be attested by eyewitnesses.

The apostles' witness is shown to have been both kerygmatic and forensic. That is, they bear witness to the saving significance of the story whose accuracy they attest, and they testify when they are accused by civil or religious power. The latter part of the story of Paul brings the forensic aspect to the fore, though it is not absent from the rest of the book. In this way, Luke exploited the dual meanings of *martyrein* (to witness to, and to testify forensically that . . .).[28]

II. An Attempt to Listen For

Having tried to listen in on Luke, we must now try to hear the import of what he was saying for our own situation, an explicitly ecclesiastical one in view of the occasion for the sermon. Among the many facets of the plight of the church today is the polarization between "activists" and "evangelicals" (may these labels be anathema!). How can our text speak a word into this situation? Moreover, can it point a way to an alternative? If so, it would articulate judgment and grace into the present state of things.

Fundamental to expository preaching, as for theology in general, is the need to minimize ideology.[29] By ideology I mean preaching and "doing theology" in a way that supplies a rationale for what we already are or

---

27. There are, of course, other facton which intimately link Luke 1-2 with the rest of Luke–Acts, as Paul Minear has shown. "Luke's Use of the Birth Stories," in *Studies in Luke–Acts* (Paul Schubert Festschrift), ed. L. E. Keck and J. L. Martyn (Nashville: Abingdon, 1966), 111-30.

28. See Strathmann's article on *martyrein* in *TDNT* 4. So also W. Mundle, "Das Apostelbild der Apostelgeschichte," *ZNW* 27 (1928) 43.

29. I explored in somewhat more detail the problem of ideology in *A Future for the Hirtorical Jesus* (Nashville: Abingdon, 1971), 103ff. Much more needs to be done in this area.

for where we are already headed. Efforts to produce on demand a theology for revolution, a theology for joy, a theology for body, a theology for evangelism, or whatever, are regularly characterized by moves which undergird what we already know. Thereby theology is deprived in advance of a critical role, since only that is permitted to be said which sanctifies what is assumed. But hearing the text calls for discerning a critical word, one which addresses both extremes in the polarized situation.

It is especially important that *this* text be preached from its context, that is, a sermon which restricts itself to the stated words "You shall receive power" (when the Holy Spirit has come) would inevitably reinforce that wing of the church which is concerned with traditional evangelism and with "spiritual power," and this could have the effect of exacerbating the situation. On the other hand if the promise of power were heard as a promise of political influence, it would not only reinforce the opposite pole, but pervert the text, since political power is what Acts 1:6f. denied to the present.

The text itself joins religious power (the Spirit) and witness to Jesus. The question over which one muses as he tries to hear is whether and in what way this combination might address our situation. To probe this, several issues must be faced.

First, according to the text, the witnessing does not bring the Spirit in its wake but vice versa, as also the subsequent narrative shows. Does this encourage today's church to remain idle until it should experience "another Pentecost"? Only on the surface of things would this appear to be a faithful hearing and appropriating of Acts. But it would imply that what the text reports is perennially paradigmatic, just as it stands. Yet, to what degree would this be true to Luke? That he regards the early church as pace-setting for subsequent Christianity is clear enough; equally clear is his view that these particular events are unique because they pertain to the unrepeatable apostles. Luke would no more have permitted one to expect "another Pentecost" than to look for another apostolate. The sermon must not urge preparation for "another Pentecost" which would solve all our problems (the original Pentecost did not solve theirs either), nor should the sermon castigate contemporary Christians for not being like the apostles immediately after Pentecost.

Second, How shall we hear Luke's understanding of witness, interwoven as it is with the theme of eyewitness guarantee of the accuracy of the good news about Jesus? Nineteen centuries later, our relation to the apostolic tradition is quite different from Luke's. Moreover, the rise of historical consciousness and of historical criticism have undone Luke's own aim: to provide a definitive account. But for us it is but one of several modes of relating Jesus and the church; furthermore, the acids of criticism have eroded our confidence in the utter accuracy of what he tells, not only in Acts but in his Gospel as well. Consequently, simply extending his contention by arguing for the accuracy of his account would not be hearing him perceptively in our situation at all. This is especially true precisely where he was most insistent—the historical reality of the resurrection. One may perhaps grant that in his situation, asserting that the apostles ate with the risen Jesus and that Jesus himself ate fish in their presence to prove he was not a ghost (Luke 24:36–42) might have undergirded the credibility of the resurrection faith. But today, reasserting this only obscures what resurrection is all about, for whatever difficulties we have with it (and they are legion), it is clear that in no case can resuscitation be regarded as resurrection. To extend Luke's point into our situation would not preserve the credibility of the gospel but forfeit it.

How then does one bear witness to Jesus in a way that is faithful to Luke's intent? The fact that Luke insisted that witness to Jesus includes an elemental narrative of his ministry should not be denigrated, but affirmed, Bultmannian theology to the contrary notwithstanding. But what assures us of the reliability of what is narrated in the sermon? If in Luke's day this was the eyewitness motif, in ours it can be precisely the critical enterprise itself. Not that New Testament criticism can guarantee its conclusions and reconstruction of Jesus; actually it cannot achieve more than degrees of probability. Nonetheless, once a skeptical attitude with regard to the Jesus traditions is in the air (and it has been for more than a century), historical criticism is the only public means of gaining any confidence at all. Moreover, enough can be known about Jesus to make out the dimensions of his work and to suggest the quality of his life and trust. That can be preached, but not as a self-validating event; it can be preached rather as an event which demands a decision for or against such a Jesus.[30]

Third, Can the Jesus whom one delineates address the polarization in such a way as to liberate the church from its impasse? If so, then by witnessing to this Jesus the deepest concerns of both evangelical and activist can be met; besides, the more manifest becomes the church's loyalty to him—that is, the more it permits itself to be reshaped by him—the

---

30. See ibid., for a fuller treatment of these themes.

more vitality it would rediscover. The abbreviated sermon which follows indicates how this exegete-preacher sought to re-say the word in the text.

III. The Effort to Resay

Our text seems to promise what we want most: power. In times of upheaval there is always a struggle for power. The more disagreement there is about the kind of society we want, the more intense and confusing is the struggle for power. Without power we cannot change the present, and no one is content with the way things are. Because we feel hijacked by history to a destination we do not want, we need power to change course. And so we are delighted to hear that our text promises power, for power is the key to change.

But it does not promise power to everybody who wants it. The promise is made to the disciples. That also reassures us, for we regard ourselves as the heirs of the early church. But we are divided over the kind of power we want and what we want it for. The activists want the church to get political power because they see that our society can avert disaster only by making deep changes. The evangelical wants a different kind of power-the power of personal religion. Wistfully we see Pentecostalism thriving and Christians of all kinds, Catholics included, taking unexpected interest in the Holy Spirit, in faith healing, and the like. And if it were not for the hair and the beads, we would probably throw open our arms to the "Jesus freaks."

We Christians are polarized over the kind of power we want. Moreover, those who seek political power view those who want the power of personal religion as escapists who are irrelevant at best, while those who want personal spiritual power see the activists as turning religion into liberal politics and the church into a lobby. And so we dissipate our energies coping and contending with one another-like a field hospital in a war zone where the supplies are few and the wounded many, but where the staff consumes its energy in argument.

There is little doubt that our polarization is threatening the life of the church and its viability in the world. But what is the solution? How do we overcome our deep divisions and suspicions of one another?

One way is for one side to win over the other. But thank God this will not happen; but were this to be the case, the outcome would be a disaster, whichever side was victor. A second way is to live and let live.

But still, learning to live with one another and to appreciate one another is not enough. A third way is needed.

The third way of overcoming this polarization is suggested by our text: "You shall have power, and you shall be my witnesses." Our text does not simply confirm what we want by way of power, but redeems us from the corners into which we seem hellbent on painting ourselves. It redeems us by speaking of the power to be effective witnesses to Jesus. What our text has in view redeems our evangelism no less than it redeems our activism. These are audacious claims. Are they justified? Let us look at them one at a time.

The first thing to see is that our text speaks of witness to Jesus. This means that Jesus himself sets the parameters of our vision, that it is he who shapes what we are about. Our text welds the promise of power to the task of witness, and this implies that the less Jesus is the core of the witness, the less power we have. And our whole history tells us that this is true.

Bearing witness to Jesus must not be confused with arguing a theological interpretation of him, for it is Jesus himself who commands our loyalty. True, there is much about him that we cannot know, and historical study of the Gospels shows that we know for certain a good deal less than we once thought we knew. But our problem is not that we do not know enough. Our problem is that we avoid the consequences of what we *do* know about him. To come straight to the point, our polarization between evangelism and action is not found in him at all. In him, word and deed do not fall apart. This man has integrity. His words ring true to his life style and his life style supports his words. Each illumines the other. By word and by deed he brought the claim and the power of the righteous reign of God to bear on the whole of man and he brought it to bear on all sorts of men. This Jesus did not announce office hours when he would be available to discuss the grace of God; rather, by consorting with the godless and with the godly, he became the grace of God to them, and so put into action the point that the Kingdom of God calls both to repent. Nor did he show any interest in making sinners more spiritual or in making Pharisees more secular. What he aimed for was turning the whole man and the whole people to God. To do this, the cripples were healed, the demon-ridden liberated, the pious confronted with the total demand of the Kingdom. Whatever each man was and whatever stood between him and a Godward life was what Jesus addressed.

LISTENING TO AND LISTENING FOR

The kind of evangelism some of us want and the kind of activism some of us demand cannot bear effective witness to this Jesus because each witnesses to but half a Jesus. Where Jesus shapes the witness, there can be no evangelism without repentance.

Somehow we have come to think that we can save souls without repentance. We have come to think that repentance is feeling sorry for not being religious sooner, that repentance is something sinners go through on the way to salvation. But repentance is turning one's whole life toward the will and way of God, and so repentance is not the preliminary step to something else but the name of the game. Repentance is the discipline of rebuilding life in alignment with the will of God.

But where did we get the notion that repentance was for only a piece of life? We cannot redeem life without redeeming everything that makes a life what it is. How can "I" be saved if what makes me who and what I really am remains untouched? And what makes me who I really am? Does it not include the whole network of relationships to my family, my neighbors, the government, the economy? Have not the injustices that prevail between blacks and whites, rich and poor, weak and strong helped make me who I really am? I see no way that the real self and the whole self can be redeemed without redeeming me at every point where I am in bondage to this world. But for some reason many Christians continue to think that it is enough to be charitable to the victims of poverty, disease, capitalistic competition, racism, and war, and not deal with the causes. That's "meddling in politics," we are told.

To redeem the whole man requires us to deal with those forces in society that put persons in need of this manifold redemption in the first place. There can be no evangelism for persons that does not call also for changing our society. When Jesus shapes the scope of evangelism in our time, nothing is immune from redemption and repentance. True, he led no marches into Pilate's office, organized no pickets. But he did not live in a time or place where citizens had responsibility for the world they lived in. To appeal today, in our situation, to what Jesus did not do then in his is to help maintain the status quo in the name of Jesus. Let us not be confused by the charge of mixing politics and religion. The fact is that they are already mixed whenever one appeals to Jesus in order to forestall criticism and reconstruction. Is Carl MacIntire less political than the Berrigans? A few years ago, a cardinal sanctified the Vietnam War by calling troops "soldiers of Christ." And how many Protestant pulpits have blessed this ghastly war in their own way? No, evangelism under the aegis of Jesus seeks to redeem the whole man and to redeem him from what made him who he is; it does not call for us to begin to mix politics and religion. It calls for us to change that damning mixture we already have.

To bear witness to Jesus redeems us from continuing an evangelism that is already discredited in the world. To bear witness to Jesus today requires us to leave no precincts of our lives untouched. Bearing witness to Jesus will therefore overcome our polarization because in this man we cannot choose between a redeeming word aimed only to the heart, and a redeeming deed aimed at the society that makes us who we are.

Bearing witness to Jesus will also redeem Christian activism from shallowness, and from the worship of political power; it can also renew the activist himself.

If the conservative evangelical sells the gospel short by restricting its scope to the inner life, the liberal activist sells it short by concentrating the need for redemption on structures and institutions. This leads to a worship of power and of politics as the key to everything. In our own time, we have seen fantastic hopes placed on political solutions to social problems, and no one can deny that changing laws and enforcing them has brought a measure of relief from the evils of racism. But now we face the spectre of another set of laws designed to call a halt. Why this running tide of reaction, symbolized by a school bus? Is it not the case that in our concern for changing laws we have not paid enough attention to changing persons? Would there be this massive resistance to bussing if we had not only enforced the law of the land but had also converted the hearts of persons as well? A thousand illustrations come to mind that laws can do only what the will and attitude of the public permits them to do.

Of all the institutions in our society, none is more directly involved in the renewal of the mind and heart than is the church. Precisely because we are in the redemption business, if I may speak that way just now, we have an unavoidable obligation to redeem the hearts and wills of persons so that laws for justice and equity are supported. Besides, do not persons write laws and administer them? Where shall we find legislators and administrators with the vision and courage to risk themselves if we neglect the message of the gospel to the hearts and wills of persons?

If we take our bearings from Jesus and bear witness to him, we shall not make politics the savior of men. Politics becomes the idol of the activist when he thinks that here lies the solution of all our ills. Laws and politics alone cannot command the obedience of the heart and will, cannot generate the commitment to be a neighbor and a brother. That comes from deep inside, from the heart of man. This is why there can be no truly effective political solutions without the redemption of the hearts of persons. Just as an evangelism without action is ineffective, so action without redemption for the heart has no future.

This brings us to another aspect of the matter—the inner power of the active Christian himself. What sort of passion produced this Christian activist in the first place, and what sustains him? A basic sense of justice and a sense of outrage in the face of injustice, to be sure. But in case after case, these persons have their roots in a heritage where the gospel reached them as persons. Probe deeply enough and you often come upon a religious commitment, a conversion experience or something like it, which set them on their way. Why must Christian activism be tongue-tied in this respect? Who is it that taught us that the decisive question is not, "Who is my neighbor?" but "How am I to be a neighbor?" Who is it that has made us guilty with acts of war? Who made us restless with the quest for wealth alone? Was it not Jesus and the gospel? Having power to bear witness to Jesus means recovering the ability to say this unabashedly; it does not mean parading our religious experience or chattering about it.

But there must be something to confess. Unless personal faith is nurtured, we shall not produce men with adequate commitment for the future. Sociology cannot generate this ability to invest one's life on behalf of justice and peace, but Jesus and the gospel can. Because the road to justice and peace is long and the battles fierce, we need a neverending stream of persons empowered by Jesus to do the job.

Moreover, without witness to Jesus and the gospel, Christian activism ceases to be Christian at all. It is perfectly true that Christians join hands with Jews, humanists, and atheists in order to gain reform of prisons or population control. But more is involved than making sure Christians do their share. They must also do their thing. What is at issue is whether Jesus and the gospel give shape and content to their participation. It is also true that there is no such thing as Christian birth control or Christian ecology, just as I do not have in view a church-dominated society. That is out of the question. What is in the question is this: When Christians join with others in pursuit of particular objectives, what do they have to contribute precisely as Christians? Unless some aspect of the gospel and its Jesus gives shape to what we do and say in social affairs, we shall end up bearing witness primarily to ourselves, by showing the world that *we* at least are where the action is. If the Christian bears no witness to the Christian values, speaks no word of warning against the idolatry of power, against the "good guys and bad guys" mentality, this activist may turn out to be just as irrelevant in his context as is the silent Billy Graham in the White House.

And so it is that our text can redeem Christian participation in public affairs from sliding into a colorless humanism, just as it can redeem evangelism from being a gaudy recruitment exercise. It can do this by redeeming us from bearing witness to half a Jesus and to half a gospel. Let diversity flourish, but let polarization disappear as we find again the meaning of full witness to Jesus. And in this full witness we shall find one another.

But our text does not promise that this redemption from polarization will come simply when we understand more clearly the nature of the gospel in the world. Rather, our text promises this renewal when we receive the power of God's presence. Do we then muddle along until this power comes to us out of the blue? Are we to yearn for "another Pentecost" before things move in a different direction? I think not, because we need to bear in mind one fundamental difference between our situation and that of the disciples between Easter and Pentecost. They never yet had this power, but we are among those who had it and lost it. The fact that they had to cool their heels in Jerusalem until power came does not require us to sit around waiting for another Pentecost just like theirs.

What I am suggesting is that we may find this power where we lost it—at the place where we began separating word from deed. What I am suggesting is that when we begin to combine them once again, when our witness to the power of the gospel to save persons begins to include a witness that remodels the world, and when our effort to reshape the world includes forthright witness to Jesus as the one in whose name we struggle, power will be there. Has it not been true again and again that there was strength necessary for this task? Who has ever complained that in giving effective witness he had to stand alone without God's empowering presence?

In any case, if we shall be renewed, if we shall receive power, it will be on the job, bearing witness to Jesus by word and by deed. The future belongs to that form of Christianity which redeems persons and which remodels the world. The gospel can still do both.

PART 2

The Presence of the Prior Word

The often repeated observation, "Christianity is an historical religion," ceases to be a cliché when it is taken as seriously as it deserves to be. Not only is Christianity *about* certain segments of ancient history, but it also *has* a history because it emerged *within* a specific history. While this is true of other religions as well, what matters here is discerning the appropriate attitude toward the early Christian past. In each of the four lectures that follow, some aspect of that past prompts reflection about Christianity's future as well.

The first two lectures were given to participants, clergy and lay folk, in the Millenium Journey (from Athens to Jerusalem) in 2000, sponsored by the World Methodist Evangelism Institute. The first lecture cautions against regretting Greek influence on early Christianity; the second declines to idealize the earliest form of the faith. The third lecture, dealing with the Apostle Paul, was first given as the Rising Lecture at the United Methodist Church in Pittsburg, Kansas in 1987, and during the next year in various colleges from Buffalo to Walla Walla, as well as to a Congregational church in Naples, Florida.

The fourth was part of a series of public lectures at Rutgers University concerning views of death in ancient and modern religions.

INTRODUCTION TO PART 2

These lectures were published as *Death and Afterlife*.[1] It is included here as published.

---

1. Hiroshi Obayashi, ed., *Death and Afterlife*, Perspectives of World Religions (New York: Greenwood, 1992).

3

Challenged by the Greek Precedent

How we will profit from our journey depends, in large part, on our stance toward what we see and recall. Our visits to Athens, Corinth, Ephesus and Patmos help us visualize the places that are important in the New Testament; they become real for us. And our visit to Eleusis reminds us that only part of the world of early Christianity appears in the New Testament. This is only the beginning. We will profit more if we see the precedents in the past that challenge us for our own time.

If we are to see the past as challenging precedent, we should set aside two other ways of regarding it. The one regards Greco-Roman civilization, and especially its religions, as the "background" of early Christianity. Calling it "background" treats that world as a stage setting, as a backdrop for the action that interests us. But as background, as stage setting, we miss the ways real people discovered the consequences of believing the gospel in their world. Instead of looking at their culture as the "background," we should see it as the *foreground*, the real world in which the Christian faith made an impact, and in which it had a future, a future that we inherited.

The other stance that should be set aside is the common regret that Christianity became part of that world, that it was Hellenized. The Hellenization of the Christian faith actually began very early, before Paul's mission. It began when Greek-speaking Jews, the Hellenists of the Book of Acts, became believers, and it continued when all sorts of Greek-using gentiles accepted the faith; it came to full tide when it became necessary to understand the person and work of Christ in terms derived from Greek philosophy. Some have celebrated this whole development as the

PART 2: THE PRESENCE OF THE PRIOR WORD

remarkable triumph of Christianity; others have lamented it as the fall of the church.

This attitude lies behind efforts to restore Christianity as it was in the beginning, before it was Hellenized. It appears in the insistance that we must get back to a simple, untheological Jesus and away from the complicated theology of Paul, Hebrews and the Nicene Creed. This view has been strong especially in American Christianity. Indeed, our third President, Jefferson, wrote that he was hoping for the "euthanasia for Platonic Christianity and its restoration to the primitive simplicity of its founder."[1] But no one can repeal history, nor was Jesus as simple as simple people think.

So where does that leave us? If we take seriously the Greco-Roman culture as the foreground of early Christianity, as the world into which the gospel was taken, and where it was changed while changing the world around it, then we are prepared to profit from that precedent. And that is what these remarks want to convey, and in three steps. The first emphasizes the differences between that world and our own; the second concerns the differences between the religions of that world and early Christianity; the third draws a few inferences.

I

I want to call attention to some features of daily life that have largely disappeared, but that are important if we are to visualize those who heard the gospel in the Greco-Roman cities.

To begin with, cities like Ephesus were very crowded. A recent estimate gives the following population figures for ca. 100 CE: Rome: 650,000; Alexandria, 400,000; Ephesus 200,000; Antioch, 150,000; Corinth, 100,000, Caesarea Maritima, 45,000, and Athens a mere 30,000.[2] These figures do not include the suburbs. The city proper was usually small, originally surrounded by a wall; inside it, much of the space was used for public places like temples and theaters. According to one estimate,[3] Antioch had 75,000 persons per squire mile or 117 per acre, whereas

---

1. Quoted in Jonathan Z. Smith, *Drudgery Divine: On the Comparison of Early Christianities and the Religions of Late Antiquity*, Chicago Studies in the History of Judaism (Chicago: University of Chicago Press, 1990), 2.

2. Rodney Stark, *The Rise of Christianity: A Sociologist Reconsiders History* (Princeton: Princeton University Press, 1996), 131.

3. Ibid., 149.

New York has about 37 per acre; Corinth had 137 per acre, more than Calcutta with 122.

Many, if not most, people lived in wooden tenements no more than 5 stories high, many consisting of but one room. As late as the fourth century AD, there were only 1800 private houses in Rome, but over 46,000 tenement houses—1 house to 25 apartments.[4] As is still true everywhere, those who had more wealth had more space, and the very wealthy had large houses and villas, often in the suburbs. The main streets were not very wide; the widest in Rome was only 21 feet,[5] and most were narrow alleys. There were no street lights in these passageways either. The tenements had no fireplaces or chimneys; windows were covered with cloth or skins. The beautiful public baths were not used much, if at all, by ordinary poor folk, and there was no such thing as soap; the tenements had no toilets, and water had to be carried. Life expectancy was about 30 years, less for girls because many of the girl babies were thrown out or exposed to elements. Disease was common, and epidemics occurred from time to time, cutting down the population.

Christianity took root in such cities. More than that, the Christians ultimately made urban life more humane, not because they deliberately set out to do so but because of how they lived. Here is what a current sociologist says: "To cities filled with the homeless and impoverished, Christianity offered charity as well as hope. To cities filled with newcomers and strangers, Christianity offered an immediate basis for attachments. To cities filled with widows and orphans, Christianity provided a new and expanded sense of family. To cities torn by violent ethnic strife, Christianity offered a new basis for social solidarity. And to cities faced with epidemics, fire and earthquakes, Christianity offered nursing service."[6] During two great epidemics, one in the middle of the second century, the next a century later, Christians did not flee, but took care of the sick, and not only their own, and so many developed immunity. As a result, more Christians survived than pagans. And because all life was precious, they did not get rid of the girl babies, and so gradually changed the proportion of men and women. So Rodney Stark (see n. 2).

---

4. Rowan A. Greer, *Broken Lights and Mended Lives: Theology and Common Life in the Ancient Church* (University Park: Pennsylvania State University Press, 1986), 94.

5. Ibid.

6. Stark, *The Rise of Christianity*, 161.

PART 2: THE PRESENCE OF THE PRIOR WORD

II

The religious scene was both different from our own and in some ways rather similar. Christianity was one of several religions that moved westward into the Greco-Roman world, which already had an oversupply of gods, temples, and religious activities. If Ephesus had had a newspaper, its Religion Section would have looked rather like the church page in our metropolitan papers. The Ephesus Times would have listed many temples, such as those of Dionysius, Isis, Demeter, Artemis, Serapis—all aspects of what Ramsey MacMullen called "the shapeless profusion of paganism."[7] The role of the temples in society was not altogether different from the role that our religion plays. Some aspect of religion touched everything, for there was no wholly secular society.[8] Nor are we as secularized as we sometimes think. Our money refers to God, our elected officials take the oath of office with a hand on the Bible, our institutions have chaplains, and in some places high school football teams pray before the game (that is, before the recent Supreme Court decision!). The ancients would have understood all this interest in the public aspects of religion. Then too, some people went along with the public worship of the gods even though they themselves were not devout believers. Ancient society too had its secular folk. Seneca spoke for many when he wrote, "As for all this obscure throng of gods, assembled through long years of ancient superstition, we shall invoke them but with the reservation in mind that their worship belongs rather to custom than truth."[9] The gods are to be respected, never slighted,[10] for honoring them assures the well being of the city and society.

There were as many different kinds and sizes of temples and shrines then as there are different kinds of churches today. But the temples had various functions that we might find strange. They often served as the bank, a safe place to put money. Many had libraries,[11] and theaters,[12] gardens and groves of trees,[13] as well as kitchens and picnic areas. Here, in

---

7. Ramsey MacMullen, *Paganism in the Roman Empire* (New Haven: Yale University Press, 1981), 5.

8. Ibid., 40.

9. Ibid., 64.

10. Ibid., 2.

11. Ibid., 11.

12. Ibid., 18, 22.

13. Ibid., 35.

the presence of the gods, people would share a meal with friends (dinner on the grounds). Only the wealthier folk had houses large enough for separate dining rooms. Temples had altars where sacrifices were burned, whether animals, birds or grains. There were choirs and dancers, as well as priests and priestesses. Public processions were common, in which images of the god were paraded. Feasting and drinking, sometimes for days, were an important part of ancient religion. There were no such things as congregations (except for the Jews). One might prefer one god or temple to another, but there was nothing to join. The priest would advocate his particular god, but there was no real pagan "evangelism"[14]—nor Jewish for that matter, though Jews did welcome others to their synagogues, where many accepted Jewish beliefs but not practices.

Alongside this public religion were the mystery religions, of which Eleusis was the most famous. It is difficult to get a clear picture of them because their ceremonies were secret, occuring usually at night. At Eleusis these observances had three elements: the story of the god was recited, statues of the god or gods were shown, and the myth was dramatized[15]—we might call it a sound and light show. The mysteries were very ancient, and offered intense personal religious experience. In the mystery initiation, for which one had to prepare with various disciplines, one made contact with divine power which purified and redeemed from ordinary life and probably made one immortal. One could be initiated into more than one mystery. Aristotle said that in the mystery initiation, one does not learn something but experiences something. Walter Burkert points out that the mystery experience was not a matter of public life but an option, like going on a pilgrimage. The mysteries offered salvation here and now and blessedness in the hereafter. The initiates tended to form communities, like clubs.[16] Initiation was often expensive; it was not a poor person's religion.

There was yet a third element in the religious scene—the worship of the emperor. That the ruler represented the gods was an old idea, and in Egypt the Pharaohs had long been seen as the divine embodied. The Roman senate came to honor as a god the emperor who had just died, but in

---

14. Ibid., 99.

15. Marvin Meyer, *The Ancient Mysteries: A Sourcebook; Sacred Texts of the Mystery Religions of the Ancient Mediterranean World* (San Francisco: Harper & Row, 1987), 10ff.

16. Walter Burkert, *Ancient Mystery Cults* (Cambridge: Harvard University Press, 1987), 10, 16, 21, 32.

the 90s Domitian was called "lord and god" during his lifetime. The point of emperor worship was to acknowledge him as the one who held the whole world together, like a god. Those who wanted to get ahead promoted this adoration, because it ensured the well-being, power, and stability of the empire. Any sign of disrespect to a god, including the emperor, was a mark of disloyalty which, if contagious, would threaten the well-being of the city. According to a recent study,[17] around 90 CE, Ephesus led the way in emperor worship, for here was built a new large temple in honor of all the emperors of the Flavian family, including Domitian. It is possible that John was exiled to Patmos for speaking against this; his book, in any case, regards the worship of Rome, and of the emperor, as Satanic.

In such a culture, Christianity appeared rather strange in some ways. In 1 Thessalonians Paul reminds the new Christians that they "turned to God from idols to serve a living and true God"—that is, instead of respecting all the gods while preferring one, or seeing them as various expressions of the one god behind them all (both views were known), they rejected them all and looked to the one true God who was none of them and differed from all of them. Only the Jews were so exclusive. Paul continues: "and to wait for his Son from heaven, whom he raised from the dead, Jesus who delivers us from the wrath to come." What a strange idea! The Greeks knew very well that humans angered the gods, and usually paid for it, but that the avenging God's own Son was expected to rescue people from his Father's wrath—why would anyone believe that? Paul knew why he could write that the gospel is foolishness to the Greeks.

Not only did Christians believe strange things while denying the gods, but their new religion seemed to be no religion at all. Later people said they were atheists—god deniers. Compared with the mystery religions, they had no secret rituals; compared with the temples, they had no statues of Jesus or God, and they had no processions when such images could be carried through the streets for public relations, and no public feasts to attract followers. In fact, they had no temples or sacred groves, no altars and no sacrifices, and no priests to preside at them. Like clubs and societies at the time, they met in homes—indicating that at least some of them had houses that would accommodate the group. They ate together, but not at the temple grounds. They emphasized service to one another and to others as well. And they stayed in touch with similar

---

17. Helmut Koester, ed., *Ephesos, Metropolis of Asia: An Interdisciplinary Approach to Its Archaeology, Religion, and Culture*, Harvard Theological Studies 41 (Valley Forge, PA: Trinity, 1995).

groups in other cities, for they understood themselves to be a new people without being an ethnic group like the Jews.

Christianity arrived in the Greco-Roman cities with three things that were distinctive, and in the long run decisive. First of all, it came with the gospel—the news of what God had done in the event of Jesus, capped by cross and resurrection. According to Acts 17, when Paul spoke to some philosophers in Athens they thought he was introducing foreign gods, as others had done, because he preached Jesus and resurrection, for they took the feminine Greek word for resurrection—*anastasis*—to refer to a person, as if Paul were talking about Jesus and Anastasia. Paul, of course, was talking about an event that signified the meaning of Jesus. The point is, the gospel came as an announcement of what had happened, is happening, and will happen soon. And all three aspects of that event were the act of God by which the world is being redeemed, and those who believed it were part of that redemption.

Second, Christianity arrived with a sense of church, a new community into which believers were baptized and so received the Spirit. They formed congregations that met regularly for celebration and instruction. They met in the houses owned by persons of means and social standing who could provide such space. When Paul arrived in Philippi this occurred in the house of a business woman, Lydia; in Corinth it was in the house of Titius Justus, who lived next to the synagogue where Paul had worn out his welcome. In time there were several house churches in a city, but they were all part of the same church in which each person was brother or sister to the others—what sociologists call a "fictive kinship group." Often whole households converted at the same time—parents, children, relatives, employees, slaves. Early Christian texts emphasis hospitality; frequently the travelers would carry letters, or become travelers in order to carry the letters.

Third, with Christianity came a new interpretation of the Greek Bible. Where there were synagogues, the Greek Bible had already arrived, but Christians insisted that its real meaning was now clear in light of God's act in Jesus. The extent to which the new Christian groups had their own copies is far from clear, for copies of the whole Bible were expensive. In any case, the Greek Bible was the only scripture they had until Paul's letters were read regularly, and the gospels began to appear. In the second century, Christian writers quote it repeatedly.

These three—the gospel message about Jesus (including his expected coming in glory), a network of communities, and the Greek Bible formed a mutually supporting unity which took root and developed in quite different directions. So much so that already at the end of the first century, there are warnings against abuses and soon the word "heresy" would appear. This appearance was inevitable, because when a faith emphasizes confession, truth must be distinguished from error because the confession expresses a conviction about what is true. Moreover, the new Christians did not enter the community with heads emptied of everything they had thought and valued before; baptism did not wash Hellenism out of their lives. It has been like that again and again whenever people in a different culture accept the gospel. What historians call the Hellenization of Christianity, today's missiologists call "indigenization." Without indigenization, any religion that enters a different culture will remain an exotic import. Just as the early Christian faith was Hellenized in the Greco-Roman world, so it was Americanized in the so-called New World, and is being Africanized and Nipponized today. That's what makes it possible to talk of precedent.

III

What, then, does it mean to be challenged by the early Greek precedent? What happened then that summons us to today? To put the question that way is to recognize that not everything that occurred then should be repeated today even if it were possible. Nonetheless, given the state of American Christianity, especially in some of its Protestant forms, some features of the early Greek precedent do challenge us to learn from the past.

The first thing is their astounding confidence in the comprehensive truth of the gospel. It seems not to have occurred to them to think, like Seneca, that the faith does not concern the truth. Nor did they regard the Christian faith as a resource for making life more satisfying, more fulfilling, or useful in improving urban life, because being Christian was often a costly affair. They would be shocked by our preoccupation with the present, for their eyes were on eternity. A mid-second century writing known as *2 Clement* gives a clear example. "We are being trained by the life which now is, that we may gain the crown in that life which is to come. None of the righteous has attained reward quickly, but waits for it; for if God should pay the recompense of the righteous speedily, we should immediately be training ourselves in commerce and not in godliness; for we should seem to be righteous when we were pursuing not piety but gain" (20:3-4). Today, those who have given up on eternity, find Paul's words rather odd. He wrote, "we look not at what can be seen but at what cannot be seen; for what can be seen is temporary, but what cannot be seen is eternal" (2 Cor 4:18). They turn this around, "we look not at what cannot be seen but at what can been seen, for what cannot be seen is uncertain and probably unreal, but what can be seen is real even if it is temporary." Where this attitude prevails, it is not surprising that the sense of urgency, of ultimacy, has declined, and with it the conviction that the gospel is the heart of the truth that exceeds its immediate utility.

In calling attention to their confidence in the truth of the gospel I am neither advocating arrogance nor calling for an objectivist epistemology that ignores the cultural relativity of all our knowledge, for Paul reminds us that now we see in a mirror dimly, and that our present knowledge is both partial and provisional. But I am struck by the fact that in the same epistle Paul did not hesitate to appropriate Greek Stoic thought and language when he wrote that "for us there is one God, the Father, from whom are all things and for whom we exist, and one Lord Jesus Christ, through whom are all things and through whom we exist" (1 Cor 8:6).

So, too, Colossians says that "Christ is the image of the invisible God, the first born of all creatures" and that "all things were created through him and for him" (Col 1:15, 20), and Hebrews asserts that the Son of God was the one "through whom he [God] created the world," the one who is the radiation of the glory of God; and then John actually says what the others imply—that the Logos of God, the self-expression of God that was the means of creation, actually became flesh and lived among us as Jesus. It was not the Jesus of Nazareth who created the world, but the Logos who became Jesus. The Hellenized Jews had already used such Greek ideas to interpret scripture and the one God, and the Greek Christians did the same to interpret Christ in relation to God. It would be several centuries before the Greek theologians worked this out theologically, but they did not shun the task by settling for "meaningful experiences." Later, the Latins, like Thomas Aquinas, found a way to state the truth of the gospel by relying on Aristotle. Today, the concept of truth itself has been called into question, so the task of rethinking what that word means is enormously complex. But the task cannot be avoided or replaced by a mere functionalist understanding of our faith, useful though that perspective can be. I accent the concern for truth because I am persuaded that unless those who teach and preach the Christian faith are convinced that what they say touches the truth, we cannot expect Christian thinkers to take up the task or Christian believers to take up the cross.

In the second place, we are challenged by the observation that the same early Greek church that laid claim to the best philosophy of the day to assert the truth of the gospel, also forged an identity, an ethos, a style of life that differed from the society around it. Those Christians did not begin by insisting that they would be "countercultural;" they became counter-cultural because their allegiance to the faith produced an identity that often *was* countercultural. If their faith made them theologically audacious, their faithfulness made them morally tenacious as well. It is easy for us to criticize them for accepting slavery, and for urging the Christian slaves to obey their masters and masters not to mistreat the slaves. We can feel morally superior to Ignatius, the early second century bishop from Antioch for writing this: "Do not be haughty to slaves, either men or women Yet do not let them be puffed up, but let them rather endure slavery to the glory of God, that they may obtain a better freedom from God. Let them not desire to be set free at the church' s expense, that they may not be found slaves of desire [*epithumia*]" (*To Polycarp* 4, slightly modified). But that is not the whole story, for a few decades earlier, the writing we call *1 Clement* says, "We know that many among ourselves have given themselves to bondage that they might rescue others. Many have delivered themselves to slavery, and provided for others with the price they got for themselves" (55). Even if we were to take out a second mortgage so we could feed the hungry, we would still fall short of that. And what will our successors in centuries to come say about our uncritical acceptance of Western individualism and social contract ecclesiology? The same Ignatius wrote to the Romans while on his way there to be martyred, "Only pray for me for strength, both inward and outward, that I may not merely speak but also have the will, that I may not only be called Christian but may also be found to be one . . . Christianity is not the work of persuasiveness but of greatness when it is hated by the world." It's hard to be more countercultural than that.

Their different ethos was nurtured especially by worship in which they not only celebrated the truth of the gospel but also participated in the victory of God; At least Ignatius thought so. Here is what he wrote to the Ephesians: "For when you gather together frequently the powers of Satan are destroyed, and his mischief is brought to nothing, by the concord of your faith. There is nothing better than peace, by which every war in heaven and on earth is abolished" (*To the Ephesians* 13). Is it accidental that the book of Revelation has the saints in heaven sing the hymns of the church on earth? How our worship services would be changed if we were convinced that something ultimate and decisive is happening!

The third way in which we are challenged by the ancient Greek precedent is by their persistent reference to Jesus, not only as the savior but also as the model for life that must endure suffering. Given the perpetual chattering in and out of today's church, I find Ignatius suggestive when he wrote, "It is better to be silent and be real, than to talk and be unreal . . . He who has the word of Jesus for a true possession can also hear his silence, that he may be perfect, that he may act through his speech and be understood through his silence . . . Let us therefore do all things as though he were dwelling in us, that we may be his temples and that he may be our God in us" (*To the Ephesians* 15). And *2 Clement* urges, "Let us, then, not merely call him Lord, for this will not save us . . . So then, brethren, let us confess him in our deeds, by loving one another, by not committing adultery, by not speaking against one another, nor by being jealous, but by being self-controlled [note the use of self-control, an important virtue in Greek morality], merciful, godly, and we ought to sympathize with each other, and not be lovers of money. By these deeds we confess him, and not by the opposite kind." *Didache* 6 (late first or early second century) knows that following Jesus' word is not easy, for it says, "For if you can bear the whole yoke of the Lord, you will be perfect, but if you cannot, do what you can." This is more than a concession, for "do what you can" urges real effort. Who knows what we can do if we do all that we can? In any case, they did not conclude that because Jesus had done so much by his death they need not do much of anything. In struggling to be real Christians in Greek cities, they indeed Hellenized Christianity, but eventually, they also Christianized Hellenism—at least in part. Their achievements were not without flaws. Nonetheless, their precedent is impressive, and it challenges us to do as well.

4

Energized by Jewish Beginnings

My previous presentation implied that we are not here in Jerusalem to detoxify our Christian faith by ridding it of its Greek elements in order to return to what was purest because it is the oldest. There was no golden age to which we should return, even if that were possible. The earliest form of the Christian faith was thoroughly Jewish, but that does not make it the golden age. It is quite likely that we would not feel at home in the earliest Jerusalem church, and those Christians would not feel comfortable with us gentile Christians either. So what are we doing here?

Just as our visits to Athens, Corinth and Ephesus help us visualize the mission of Paul and the small house churches that resulted, so our visits to Galilee and Jerusalem help us visualize Jesus as a figure in his own time and place. Despite many changes in this land, the land itself—the hills, the Sea of Galilee, the wilderness of Judea, the Jordan—remains, and reminds us that God's redemptive act did not occur "once upon a time" in some imagined place, but in a real time and in real places. We can see some of what Jesus also saw, walk where he too walked, and perhaps resolve again to fall in behind him.

But at just this point it is important to remember that we do not, and cannot, have Jesus without the faith of the early church, for without that we would not even know that there was a Jesus, let alone what he was like. Nor should we forget that the Jesus who trod these roads and climbed these hills - including Skull Hill in Jerusalem—was a Jew who did not view us gentiles positively, except for the Roman army officer who asked him to heal his boy (Matt 8:5–13). Jesus' mission was to his own people, and according to Matthew, when he sent his disciples on their mission he said, "Go nowhere among the gentiles and enter no town of the Samaritans, but go to the lost sheep of the house of Israel" (Matt 10:5). It is the risen Jesus who commissions the disciples to go to us gentiles. So, given the avowed Jewishness of Jesus, what are we Christian gentiles doing here?

I suggest that we are here to be energized by the Jewish beginnings of our faith. For that to happen, we need a sense of what those beginnings looked like. That is the first step. The next two will consider what being energized by those beginnings calls for.

I

The oldest form of the Christian movement has proven to be very difficult to describe, because we have no records from those who shaped it, for it is likely that none of the New Testament was written in Jerusalem. The oldest description of the Jerusalem church, in the Book of Acts, was written at least half a century later for Christians in the Greco-Roman cities. Acts does give us very important snapshots of the Jerusalem church, but it is totally silent about groups of Jesus people in Galilee. So almost everything that can be said about the first decades is inference, and even sound inference is not evidence. Besides, many of the inferences are controversial.

An important clue about the nature of the Jerusalem church comes from a figure who was never a member of it, and who was distrusted by it—the Apostle Paul. By about AD 57, he was no longer sure he could trust that church either. At the end of his letter to the Romans he reports that before coming to Rome he will first go to Jerusalem to take the offering which his largely gentile churches had collected for the poor believers there. For Paul, this offering expressed the solidarity of gentile Christians with Jewish believers. But now he is not sure they will accept it. Why not? After all, a decade before, the Jerusalem council agreed that male gentile converts to faith in Jesus did not need to be circumcised and so become Jews. It seems that nonetheless, some Christian Jews in Jerusalem insisted that because Jesus was the Messiah, all members of the Messiah's community had to be Jews, whether by birth or circumcision. To oversimplify, those who thought this way created a Christianized Judaism as the norm for the whole church. Though Paul fought against this view, Romans shows that the issue was about to come to a head, right here in Jerusalem.

According to Acts, when Paul arrived, James told him that many Jewish believers accepted the rumor that he had told also Jewish Christians in his churches not to circumcise their children either and to abandon their Jewish customs (Acts 21:20–21). While Acts shows that the rumor was false, it also shows how unacceptable Paul was in Jerusalem: though he was in prison in Caesarea for two years, Acts says not a word about any Jewish believer coming to see him. He was persona non grata.

About the later history of the Christianized Judaism in Jerusalem we know very little. The fourth century Eusebius—who relies on second century material—reports that the leadership of the church developed a unique pattern. After Peter left, the church was headed by Jesus' brother, James, who had not been a disciple but became a believer after the risen Jesus appeared to him. Legend has it that in the temple he prayed so often that his knees got calluses like a camel's. After his death, the leadership passed from one brother to another; thereby the Messiah's family remained in charge. What happened to this community when the war against Rome broke out in 66 is disputed. There is a tradition that the church fled to Pella, east of the Jordan, but many doubt this was the case, for it is unlikely that the Romans would have permitted any Jews to escape. Perhaps a few did. In any case, the original church did not survive the war. Later groups of Jewish believers, like the Ebionites and Nazoreans, claimed to be descendants of the original church, but that too is doubtful. The Greek church regarded them as heretics because they did not agree that Jesus was the incarnation of the Son of God. One can only speculate how the Christianized Judaism in Jerusalem might have developed had the revolt against Rome not occurred.

The Christianized Judaism of the 40s and 50s was but one of several kinds of Judaism at the time. But then the first revolt against Rome changed everything. The center of the Jewish religion, the temple, was destroyed, and with it the priesthood, most of whom appear to have been Sadducees. Another group that disappeared were the Essenes at Qumran, who probably produced the Dead Sea Scrolls, and who hated the temple priesthood. Those Jews who did survive to reshape Judaism were the rabbis, who inherited the traditions of the Pharisees. Not until after the second revolt against Rome in 132–135, which was more devastating than the first, did the rabbis begin to record their traditions, beginning with the Mishnah, which in due course became the core of the Talmud. What we know as "rabbinic literature" was produced after New Testament times. By the time the Gospels were written, it is very doubtful that

Matthew or Luke ever saw a real Pharisee. If that is right, then when they wrote "Pharisee" they thought "rabbi"—the rabbi they knew in the Jewish communities that were being reshaped between the two revolts. We have no writings from the Pharisees themselves, but we have writings from two men who had once been Pharisees—one was Paul, and the other was Josephus, who switched sides during the first revolt, and then retired to Rome on a pension, where he wrote about the revolt, blaming it on Jewish hot heads. In short, it is as hard to get a clear historical picture of the Pharisees that Jesus and Paul knew as it is to get a clear historical picture of Jesus. What is clear, however, is that the Judaism that Jesus and Paul knew was much more diverse than later rabbinic Judaism, and that many Jews throughout Palestine were thoroughly Hellenized and secularized.

Fortunately, the destruction of the Christianized Judaism led by James was not the whole story, though the rest can only be surmised. Apparently there were groups of Jewish Jesus people who did not look to James but to Peter, on the one hand, and perhaps to John on the other. What these Jewish believers created can be called "Jewish Christianity," diverse as it was. Though rooted in the early Jerusalem church, it was developed especially among Greek speaking Jews of the diaspora. According to Acts, when these Hellenized Jewish believers were driven out of Jerusalem, they took the gospel to Jews and others. Apparently, the Jewish establishment could tolerate the temple-centered Christianized Judaism of James but not the Christianity of the Hellenized Jews like Stephen and Philip.

We find various expressions of this Jewish Christianity. Two New Testament examples are the Gospels of Matthew and John, and in the traditions they used; we find it also in a writing found a century ago called "The Teaching of the Twelve Apostles" or simply the *Didache*. The Gospel of John, being influenced by the theology of Hellenized Judaism, is Jewish, Greek, and Christian all at once. The same is true of Paul, though with different results because, as the apostle to gentiles, he addressed somewhat different issues posed by the law of Moses and the customs of Judaism.

For non-Pauline Jewish Christianity, on the other hand, the problem was not the law itself but the right way of understanding and obeying it in light of Jesus. So far as we can tell, these Jewish believers continued to be practicing Jews, though their way diverged more and more from the ways of the rabbis. Between the two revolts the rabbis had to contend not only with Jesus-believing Jews but also with other ways of being Jewish, especially in the diaspora. In order to consolidate Jewish life in accord with rabbinic understanding, around 85 the rabbis inserted into a synagogue prayer a curse on the *minim*, the heretics. Because deviants could not say this part of the prayer without contradicting their convictions, Jewish Christians—but not only they—found it impossible to remain part of the Jewish community controlled by the rabbis.

In short, for the Jewish Christians, the question was not whether to remain Jewish but how to do so—whether under the aegis of the rabbis or of Jesus. This choice is reflected in the Gospels; they ignore what Jesus and the Pharisees had in common and emphasize the differences, because the Jewish Christians traced their distinctive ways of being Jewish back to Jesus. The conflict was both inevitable and intensely personal because the Jesus people did not separate themselves and relocate as did the Essenes who moved to Qumran near the Dead Sea. Rather, the Christian Jews lived with other Jews in the Jewish sections of the cities. As in the villages, here any deviation produced controversy that involved also family relationships. This is reflected in Matthew 10, where Jesus says that "a man's enemies will be those of his own household." Because of their allegiance to Jesus as the promised Messiah, the Greek speaking Jewish Christians came to have more in common with gentile Christians than with their friends and relatives who followed the rabbis.

One is reminded of the Puritans and the early Wesleyans; they too did not set out to be separate, but became separate communities because their convictions and experiences made them too different to remain within the inherited tradition. In contrast with the Puritans and early Methodists, however, these Greek speaking Jewish Christians did not remain separate but became part of the larger, ever more gentile church.

The Jewish beginnings to which we gentile Christians look are those associated with Christian Hellenized Jews. Why? Because almost everything we know about Jesus depends on the Gospels, which rest on their traditions about him. Presumably, the Christian Hellenized Jews were the ones who translated the stories and sayings of Jesus into Greek; they were the ones who claimed that Jesus was more than a prophet with a message about God because he himself was the message about God, not only because God resurrected and exalted him, but also because of who he was—for Matthew, the virgin born Son of God, for Paul, John, and Hebrews, the pre-existing Son of God who became Jesus. They were the ones who saw that because of the resurrection, they must do what Jesus himself had not done, namely, take the gospel to gentiles. All this, and more, they did without forgetting that Jesus had been a Jew among Jews. They not only expected the risen Jesus to return in glory but also experienced his presence in the Spirit. They could not foresee what they set in motion, but in looking back, we can see what they accomplished, and be grateful.

We should be especially grateful for their translating the Jesus traditions, which were then written into our New Testament Gospels, for like Paul, the Gospels insist that Jesus was a Jew in a real time and place. The significance of this became evident in the second century, when some gentile Christians virtually eliminated the Jewish element from the words and deeds of Jesus (namely the Gnostics), and when Marcion went even farther and claimed that the real God sent Jesus to save the world from the creator, the god of the Jews. Because both ways of thinking keep coming back, we now know what we gentile Christians are doing here. For this new millenium, we are here to be energized by the Jewish beginnings transmitted to us by the Christian Hellenized Jews of the first century.

II

We can be energized by what energized them. And what is that? It was the conviction that God had validated Jesus by resurrecting him from the realm of the dead, thereby making him the key to the future - a conviction expressed by saying that he was now sitting at God's right hand, and that he would come to consummate what has begun. In other words, the future belongs to Jesus. And for those who shared this conviction, also the present belongs to him. And if that is the way it is, then he is the lens through which we see God, and then Jesus—his way and word—restructures the understanding of God, the relation to God, and to one another as well. In short, this conviction about Jesus, and its implications, refocused their Jewish faith and life, so that now Jesus becomes the pivot on which their lives turn, and the norm to which they know themselves accountable because he authorized it. To be sure, they left no diaries which recorded their thinking, but we do have the results in the Gospels. We should not take the Gospels, and what they express, for granted, precisely because those who wrote them did not rely on their own memories of Jesus. Therefore the whole phenomenon from Easter to the Gospels is worth pondering. Here highlights must suffice.

First, because the first believers were Jews, as was Jesus, their convictions about Jesus refocused the convictions about God, Scripture, sin and salvation, resurrection and judgment that they already had. The Easter appearances did not occur in a vacuum, and apart from Paul, they occurred only to those who had known Jesus, for only they could have known that it was he whom they saw.

Second, even though the disciples were surprised and astounded by the appearances, astonishment alone does not automatically produce a transforming conviction about the meaning of the experience, for one could simply remain baffled by it. An astonishing event acquires the power of a conviction when it rings true, when it fits some convictions already in place and challenges and changes others, and when the reconfigured convictions produce a reconfigured life. Following Daniel Patte, I speak of "convictions" deliberately, because convictions are not simply ideas we hold strongly; they are ideas that hold us. We can change ideas, but convictions change us. To say this concretely, for the disciples the appearances became convictions about Jesus because they saw a fit between the Jesus they remembered and the God who resurrected him. Otherwise, why would God have resurrected precisely Jesus and only Jesus? And it all had to fit Scripture too, and this required reading it in a new way. Luke expresses this by reporting that the resurrected Jesus himself showed them how to read scripture in light of Easter. Moreover, the new conviction about God, Jesus, and Scripture was confirmed by their own transformed lives, and especially by a new energy, the presence of God's Spirit. But even a conviction confirmed by an energized new life is not proof that will stand up in court. In short, from the start within Judaism, the Jesus people were constituted as a community by a confession of faith, and increasingly, this confession and its implications distinguished them from other Jews.

Third, the disciples were so energized by what happened to them that they told others about it so that they too might share their new convictions. Given the diversity of Judaism at the time, that is not really surprising. What is surprising, and highly significant as well, is that many people believed the news about Jesus even though they had not known him personally. How do we understand that? To be sure, those Jews who believed the first disciples also shared Jewish convictions. But that was hardly enough to make the message about the decisive significance of Jesus credible. Nor, one may assume, was the claim sufficient that the disciples had seen the resurrected Jesus, for important as that was, it is doubtful whether that alone would have made the message credible to those who had not seen him themselves. What did make the message credible to those who had not known Jesus was the fit, the coherence, between the story of God, the story of Jesus, and the story of Jesus' followers who were changed and energized. The hearers might doubt or contest the story of God or the story of Jesus, but they could not easily dispute the changed lives of the messengers because that was evident. And so the hearers became convinced believers who, also energized by the Spirit, themselves became messengers who convinced their hearers, etc. etc. In a word, the contagion of the message is inseparable from the contagion of changed messengers. And the key to it is the story of Jesus as the story of God.

Fourth, that story—by which I mean the traditions about what Jesus had said and done, told from the perspective of Easter—portrayed a figure who was thoroughly Jewish in his own way. He identified with no type of Judaism known to us. Nor did he refer to a teacher from whom he learned the will and way of God or how to interpret Scripture. With remarkable audacity, he spoke and acted for God, combining word and deed in order to point to the coming Kingdom—that event in which God would make all things right. He expelled the demons and healed the sick; he consorted with sinners of all kinds, blessed the children and accepted women into his group. His call to repentance was not a summons to prepare for the worst but a call to respond to the coming of the best, God's royal rule. The God he represented was the God of Israel, refocused through his mission which ended in an execution he did not flee. His resurrection did not suggest that God had waited to see whether he deserved it but implies that God had been at work in this remarkable life all along, and that the Jesus event was indeed God's own event. Those who told the Jesus story this way because they were changed by it, saw in Jesus' death the atoning act of God through which their sins were forgiven—a thoroughly biblical and Jewish way of thinking.

Some Christians have been so offended by the atoning significance of Jesus' death that they refuse to think in such terms and so understand Jesus' death to be like that of a martyr for a cause—perhaps not realizing that this leaves God outside the event itself. But the Jesus story in the Gospels portrays a figure who was more than a Jewish peasant whose ideas about God and whose saucy sayings got him killed; that story makes the astounding claim that the God of Israel, the creator and judge of all, was himself involved in the event called Jesus. If that claim, like the first Beatitude, is true, then nothing is the same.

And those who made this claim were not the same either. The book of Acts reports a detail that points to this change, to the fit between Jesus and his messengers. That detail comes just before the story of Peter going to Cornelius at Caesarea (Acts 10). Peter was at Joppa (Tel Aviv). Where did he stay? At the home of Simon the tanner. Tanners were at the bottom of the social pyramid because their craft entailed working with all sorts of hides and using urine. The Peter who was not ashamed to stay with Simon the tanner had been with the Jesus who was not afraid to consort with outcasts and sinners. Staying with Simon prepared Peter for what was to follow. The influence of Jesus is like that.

III

If we gentile Christians are energized by these Jewish beginnings, the new millenium holds great promise. Indeed, a great era of the Christian faith is already under way. As never before, gentiles of all colors and cultures are finding in Jesus, and the God of Israel he represents, a redeeming alternative to what they have known. As never before, gentile Christians too are calling Abraham their father. To borrow Paul's analogy in Romans 11, the wild olive grafted into the old root is taking hold all around the globe, as never before. Because Jesus was the kind of Jew he was, we gentile Christians are grafted into Abraham, not into Moses. And being grafted into Abraham, we find ourselves to be brothers and sisters of Arab and Palestinian Christians. That is one reason we are here.

At the same time, we gentile Christians who are heirs of Greek and Latin Christianity in Europe have unfinished business if we are truly energized by these Jewish beginnings. And that means first of all overcoming, as best we can, the dreadful legacy of our treatment of the Jewish people by abandoning, once and for all, the habit of putting down the Judaism of Jesus' day in order to lift Jesus up. In addition, we will not regard the Jewish beginnings of our faith as the point of departure, but as the constitutive and abiding ways of understanding the God he represented and the human condition that his life and death redeem. Whenever these Jewish roots and modes of thought are ignored or abandoned, we lapse into a gentile religion in the name of Jesus. But when we acknowledge them gratefully and affirm them vigorously, we have good news about the

God who is different because he is holy, and being holy is determined to make all things right and will not rest until the goal is reached. To do that, we must adhere to the Jesus we know through the Gospels of the Hellenized Jewish Christians; and then, like the the Greek theologians after them, we must find ways to express the theological meaning of this event cogently and live it convincingly because it is our deepest conviction. To be energized in this way is why we are here.

5

Paul: Problem and Promise

I will focus on the one person who is responsible for writing more of the New Testament than anyone else—the Apostle Paul. Much of what he said needs to be heard today. Which is to admit that I am a Paulinist, though I am not prepared to grant that he was always right or wise. Some people go farther than that. They find him to be wrong in such important things that they are not prepared to hear him at all.

So the first thing we will do is to note some of the reasons why Paul is a problem. Then we will see the man in his own time, and discover that also the scholars find Paul to be a problem, though for quite different reasons. Finally, we will note aspects of his message which are promising resources for Christian faith and life today.

Paul the Problem

A complete history of the hatred of Paul has yet to be written. It would, I am sure, tell us more about the haters than about Paul, because he is one of those powerful personalities whose strong opinions generate both deep loyalty and intense hatred. It is not alway s clear if either his friends or his foes have really understood him. Either way, Paul is a problem.

Today, vigorous objections to Paul come from those women who hold him responsible for the suppression of women in the church, and consequently in Western culture as well. After all, the First Letter to Timothy says, "Let a woman learn in silence with all submissiveness. I permit no woman to teach or have authority over men; she is to keep silent . . . And Adam was not deceived, but the woman was deceived and became the transgressor. Yet woman will be saved through bearing children" (2:11–15). And the Letter to the Ephesians says, "Wives be subject to your husbands, as to the Lord. For the husband is the head of the wife as Christ is the head of the church . . . As the Church is subject to Christ so let wives be subject in everything to their husbands" (5:22–24).

New Testament scholarship helps Paul by relieving him of the responsibility for writing these things. That is, most scholars are convinced that the Letters to Timothy and Titus were not written by Paul himself but by one of his followers, after the Apostle was dead. Many scholars have reached the same conclusion about Ephesians. That still leaves these books in the New Testament, but it does free Paul from responsibility for what others wrote in his name. Scholarship also helps Paul by showing that his attitude toward women was rather forward-looking for its time. In 1 Corinthians 7 he insists that with regard to sex the man's body belongs as much to the wife as the wife's belongs to the husband. And 1 Corinthians 11 shows that women are not silent in church. In fact, scholars have discovered evidence in Romans 16 that Paul praises a Christian leader who seems to have been a woman apostle and not a man as the translators have made her. We know the names of about as many women leaders in Paul's churches as men. But even so, he was no feminist. His language about God is consistently masculine. We can hardly expect it to be otherwise, for he was a man of his time. The real question is whether there are also passages in Paul which hold real promise for strengthening equality of women and men today.

Another group which resents Paul today is the AfroAmerican descendants of slaves. They find it hard to forget that 1 Timothy says, "Let all who are under the yoke of slavery regard their masters as worthy of all honor . . . Those who have believing masters [that is, Christian masters] must not be disrespectful on the ground that they are brethren" (6:1–2). And the Letter to Titus reads, "Bid slaves be submissive to their masters, and give satisfaction in every respect" (2:9). The same sort of thing is found in Ephesians and Colossians. Here too scholarship frees Paul from these words by concluding that he did not write these letters.

But that is not the end of the matter, because Paul said not one word against slavery itself. Indeed, he sent back to his owner a runaway slave who had become a Christian, Onesimus. And in 1 Corinthians 7 he suggests that even if a slave has the chance to become free he should remain as he is, because everyone should stay in the state in which one became a Christian. One can understand why the grandmother of Howard

Thurman, the Black preacher, vowed that she would never read any part of the Bible which Paul wrote except the chapter on love. Again, the question is whether there are other parts of Paul which hold real promise for the descendants of slaves who are still struggling for equal freedom.

Paul is a problem not only for particular groups, for we all remember that he wrote that everyone should "be subject to the governing authorities. For there is no authority except from God. Therefore he who resists authorities resists what God has appointed" (Rom 13:1–2). No wonder that monarchs justified their tyranny by speaking of "the divine right of kings."

Scholarly considerations put also this passage into perspective by pointing out that in Paul's time the state had not yet persecuted the church, as it would do later, and by reminding us that he wrote this for a Christian community whose Jewish members had been expelled from Rome because arguments over the Messiah were disturbing the Jewish quarter. But still, one wonders whether the apostle had to be so flat-footed about his support of existing political authority. Here too we ask whether there might be other passages which hold a promise of support for those who today put their lives on the line in defense of civil liberty in the face of tyranny.

In any case, the more we look at Paul, the more fascinating he becomes. After all, he has been, and continues to be, the most influential Christian of all time. That is reason enough to want to know more about him. So the next part of this lecture will sketch the man and his work; that will show why he is a problem also for scholars.

Paul and His Mission

A. Paul's Letters report far less about his life than we want to know. Only when he defends himself and his gospel does he reveal anything about his biography. To some extent we can fill in the gaps from the Book of Acts, but this must be used with care, partly because it omits whatever does not contribute to the heroic image of Paul, and partly because Acts and Paul do not always agree. Consequently, a real biography of Paul cannot be written. But we can look at important features of his life and work, guided by three questions: Who was Paul and what sort of person was he? What was the heart of his message?, and How did he go about spreading it?

1. Who was Paul? A contemporary of Jesus, but probably a few years younger. He came from Tarsus, a city on the southeast coast of modern

Turkey, where he was born into a Jewish family whose forebears were the small tribe in ancient Israel from which came its first king, Saul, after whom the newborn was named. Like many Jews in the Greco-Roman world, he also had a Latin and Greek name, and it is by this that we know him, Paulus. His family must have been fairly prominent, for according to Acts Paulus enjoyed from birth the privilege of being a Roman citizen (Acts 22:28). About his youth and education in Tarsus, a university town, we know nothing at all. As a young adult, presumably, he went to Jerusalem where he became a Pharisee, one of the major strands of Judaism at the time. As a Pharisee, he was fully committed to the Torah, which for Pharisees had two forms—the written Pentateuch and the unwritten traditions of its meanings, handed on by word of mouth from teacher to pupil, generation after generation. Long afterward, Paul remembers himself as having been a zealous, enthusiastic devotee of the Torah and Jewish tradition, who managed to live a blameless life. This model Pharisee might have become a famous Jewish rabbi like Hillel had his world not been challenged by people who claimed that the expected Messiah had already been here and was executed on a cross by Rome but raised from the dead by God.

Paul was one of those persons given to total commitment to the truth as one sees it. His was one of those minds that relentlessly penetrates to the heart of the matter, and once arrived there, finds it impossible to say "maybe." His was an either/or mind. So he could not regard the Jesus-movement as a curiosity, but resolved to stamp it out. Paul never forgot that he had once been a persecutor of the Church who had committed his energies to opposing what God was doing. He came to the Christian faith neither as a troubled soul nor as an earnest seeker but as a persecutor who became a propagator; Paul could understand this only as God's free intervention in his life. No wonder he became the theologian of the sovereign grace of God. He never saw this event as conversion from Judaism to another religion, though in retrospect we can see that this was implied; Paul saw it as the event in which God revealed to him that Jesus was the Son of God, the God-given means of keeping the promise to Abraham and of redeeming the world. As a result, the total commitment which he had once directed toward the Torah he now directed to Christ. After Paul's turn to Christianity, which took place within five years of Good Friday, the church would never be the same again, for something entered it which it could not digest without being changed. And so it has been to this very day.

PAUL: PROBLEM AND PROMISE

Paul was not an easy man to live with. He generated both deep loyalty and fierce opposition. Although the book of Acts has most of Paul's troubles come from outsiders, his Letters show that he was at odds with his own churches. Decades later the only other book in the New Testament which mentions him, 2 Peter, says, "our beloved Paul wrote to you according to the wisdom given him, speaking of this as he does in all his letters. There are some things in them that are hard to understand, which the ignorant and unstable twist . . . as they do the other scriptures" (2 Pet 3:15–16).

His letter-writing caused problems already in his life-time; in Corinth one letter left the wrong impression and had to be corrected (1 Cor 5:9–13) and another caused sorrow (2 Cor 7:8). He seems to have been sharper on paper than in person, for he admits that in Corinth people were muttering, "His letters are weighty and strong, but his bodily presence is weak and his speech of no account" (2 Cor 10:10). That comment would be more illuminating if we knew what standard they expected him to meet.

In any case, he was a many-sided person. Having the best mind in the church, he outclassed his opponents in debate. But he also worked miracles, though he barely mentions it (Rom 15:18–19). Moreover, he spoke in tongues and was proud of it (1 Cor 14:18–19), and had visions. In fact, he thought that he had some sort of malady, his "thorn in the flesh," because God wanted to keep him from being "too elated by the abundance of revelations" (2 Cor 12:9). What this "thorn in the flesh" was is anybody's guess.

Whatever it was it did not prevent him from travelling through Asia Minor and Greece, or from crossing the Aegean Sea several times, or from planning a trip that would take him from Greece to Jerusalem and then to Italy and Spain. He was a tough apostle, having endured being beaten with rods, being stoned, shipwrecked three times and once adrift at sea for a day and a night; he endured sleepless nights and foodless days (2 Cor 11:24–27).

He was proud of his accomplishments (1 Cor 15:10). He took a back seat to nobody; even if the chief apostles had big reputations he could say, "What they were makes no difference to me; God shows no partiality" (Gal 2:6), and he could refer to Peter, James, and John sarcastically as those who "were reputed to be pillars" of the church (Gal 2:9). And he could be crude to the point of saying that he wished that those who were so keen on circumcising gentiles would mutilate themselves while they were at it (Gal 5:12). On the other hand, he could be generous, warm hearted, forgiving (2 Cor 2:5–11), and tolerant of those who expressed their faith differently so long as the central message was not jeopardized (Phil 1:15–18). As a pastor he could praise as well as blame, and he could admit that he had been harsh. He was concerned for each new Christian in his churches as they tried to develop a style of life appropriate to the gospel, and his letters touch all sorts of matters from the essentials of the faith to vegetarianism and veils on women's heads. Commonly called "Saint Paul," a title he would have refused, he was a very human apostle.

2. What was the message that propelled him across mountains and seas? It was not Jesus' own message which he spread but the message about Jesus, the news of what this event called Jesus Christ, focussed on the cross and resurrection, means for the human condition in relation to God. We do not know how Paul came to his understanding of the meaning of Jesus; all we know is the conclusions to which he came. So it is not easy to think Paul's thoughts after him or to think our way back into Paul's time in order to get a sense of how his message might have been heard. That was the time before our Gospels were written, before the church had organized its clergy, and before certain doctrines like the Trinity had been hammered out. If we compare the Christianity we know with the Mississippi at New Orleans, into which have flowed the Ohio, the Missouri, and the Tennessee, then with Paul we are way upstream, near the headwaters north of Minneapolis.

The pivot on which Paul's gospel turned was the resurrection of the crucified Jesus. Now Paul believed in and hoped for resurrection long before he became a Christian, for this was one of the standard beliefs of Pharisaism, but not of all Jews. Those who accepted the idea of resurrection regarded it as one of the things that would happen at the end of history, at the end of This Age and the beginning of the Age to Come—when everything would be put right. If God resurrected Jesus then the curtain is going up on the New Age, and all of the other events expected at the end of history are about to happen. After nineteen centuries it is hard to visualize the sense of urgency which Paul's understanding of Jesus' resurrection entailed.

But not only a sense of urgency; also a sense of ultimacy, because if the New Age has begun to dawn, then everything must be looked at in light of the meaning of Jesus, whom God had installed as Lord, as Regent, by resurrection and who would soon return to complete the salvation that has now begun. Those who believed that God had resurrected

Jesus already experienced the first signs of salvation, and enjoyed the empowering presence of the Spirit of God. These believers were baptized in Christ's name, or in his authority—an idea which Paul deepened by understanding it as baptism into Christ's death, so that they were made shareholders in the one man who escaped from Death.

Other Christians believed these things too. Yet, looking back, we can see that Paul was creating something that had not existed before—a consistent, though not complete, Christian theology.

He did not set out to be the first Christian theologian, but an obedient emissary of God to the gentile world. To be sure, others too shared the good news with gentiles. But still, it was one thing to accept gentiles into the church, another thing for Paul to make a deliberate effort to bring them in, and to insist that these gentiles could be bonafide Christians without becoming Jews at the same time. Had Paul not won that battle, the Christian movement would have broken up into a Jewish sect on the one hand and a minor gentile religious movement led by Paul on the other.

3. How did Paul go about his mission? He concentrated on the cities of Asia Minor and Greece, where he often found Greek-speaking Jews like himself, and others who followed the same trade, making tents. With them he began. In contrast with many travelling teachers of the day, Paul accepted no fees from those who heard him but supported himself by working at his trade: he accepted money from one congregation, that in Philippi, but only when he was already teaching somewhere else. That made them partners in his work. Paul travelled with a small group of associates. Often he accepted the hospitality of wealthier persons who became his patrons or sponsors—as was customary in those days.

It has been common to speak of Paul's converts as coming from the lowest classes of society; that is a romantic idea without solid foundation. Rather, his people were artisans and small business people; had they been desperately poor, they would not have owned slaves. These people met in the tenements above the small shops and workplaces. Although Sunday as we know it did not yet exist, they met at least every week, on the Lord's Day, to celebrate the resurrection, to hear Paul explain the scriptures, and to eat together. Church supper and Lord's Supper were the same thing until Paul asked the Corinthians to eat supper at home first. These assemblies lasted into the night, and were marked by singing, praying, tongue speaking, teaching and fellowship. In such settings Paul's letters were first read. Paul's communities did not worry about whether to ordain women, because they did not ordain men either. Each person contributed what the Spirit enabled one to do. In these groups, Paul was a pastor, even in absentia. When problems arose after he had moved on, he wrote letters to deal with them as if he were still on the scene. In a few years, he had established a string of house churches. The significance of this should not be missed. Paul insisted that these congregations understand themselves as local expressions of the one church which had its roots in Jerusalem. In time, this church developed an organizational structure under the bishops. Other ancient religions too spread across land and sea, but so far as we can tell, only Christianity organized itself and viewed itself as the church catholic. That it could do so is due, in no small measure, to the foundation laid by Paul.

B. The more we ponder Paul's place in early Christianity, the more we discover that scholars too have problems with Paul, of which I shall mention only four.

1. What was Paul's role in the development of early Christianity? In Paul's day, the Christian movement swiftly changed from being a small sect within Judaism to a trans-cultural religious phenomenon in the Greco-Roman world. Before long, the majority of Christians were gentiles who brought into the church a quite different background, and quite different religious sensibilities from those of the earliest Jewish believers in Jerusalem. Scholars call this invasion of the Greek factor the "Hellenization of Christianity" and some regard it as the most important development since Pentecost. Even if that were an exaggeration, the question remains: What was Paul's role in this Hellenization process? This question is important because people have quite different views of Hellenization. Those who regard it as Christianity's fortunate emancipation from its original Jewish limitations see Paul the Hellenizer as the hero; but those who think the Greek influence caused Christianity to betray its Jewish roots, see Paul the Hellenizer as the villain. Today, most scholars regard both views as too extreme, because the Hellenization of Christianity was not the work of Paul alone; it began when Greek-using Jews became Christians. In any case, the question of Paul's place in early Christianity remains a problem for scholarship.

2. The second problem concerns the relation between the Letters of Paul and the book of Acts, because Acts not only gives a rather different picture of Paul from what we find in the Letters. Acts views the time of the Apostles as the Golden Age, when the church was generally free from internal problems, and the ones that did arise were settled agreeably. This

means that both Acts and the Letters give us onesided views of Paul, Acts because it allows no controversies between Paul and his churches, the Letters because most of them deal with controversies. Nor can we compensate for this double one-sidedness by simply combining Acts and the Letters. That would be like trying to get a full picture by combining half a photograph with part of an oil portrait. Even though we must rely on Acts for much of what we know about Paul, it is his Letters that are the primary sources because they put us in touch with the man himself.

3. Third, the Letters pose problems of their own, beginning with uncertainty about which of the 13 Letters that claim Paul as the author were actually written by him. Seven of them are surely genuine: Romans, 1 & 2 Corinthians, Galatians, Philippians, 1 Thessalonians, and Philemon. They provide the solid foundation for the modern understanding of Paul. The others show how he was understood later. Their religious value does not depend on whether Paul wrote them. They are just as much a part of the New Testament as the genuine Letters. Moreover, some of the Letters we have actually combine two or more letters of which Paul wrote, so that the seven might represent as many as a dozen letters, though here scholarship is far from united. Now, if some of our Letters combine earlier letters, and if each letter was a response to a particular situation, then his thought was always in motion. Each time he wrote he said only what he judged necessary to say. He never says everything he thinks about a subject, but always assumes a great deal. Consequently, it is difficult to create a fully consistent statement of what Paul thought.

4. The most vexing problem of Paul is his relation to Jesus. Why does he say so little about him or his teachings? Paul never mentions a single deed in Jesus' ministry. He is concerned only with Jesus' birth, passion (including the Lord's Supper) and resurrection. Even when Paul seems to have Jesus' teachings in mind, he does not mention Jesus. Moreover, what was basic to Jesus, the Kingdom of God, is marginal to Paul, and what is important for Paul—Sin and Death as enslaving powers from which one must be redeemed—is at best only implied in Jesus' thought. At the same time, Paul regards Jesus as the pivotal event through which God acted to redeem the world. How can Paul make so much of Jesus and yet say so little about his life and ministry? Naturally, scholars have proposed all sorts of solutions to this problem: that his letters assume information about Jesus; that he really did not know much about Jesus; that he was so interested in the resurrected Lord that he was indifferent to what Jesus had said and done before the crucifixion. In any case Paul did

not see himself as a disciple of Jesus but as an apostle, whose task it was to announce the significance of what God had achieved in Jesus.

The real question, of course, is whether this apostle's thought holds any significant promise for us today.

Paul's Promise

The best way to discover the promise of Paul is to expose oneself to his thought as one struggles with the big issues. Then one finds that he deepens our thinking and challenges our assumptions. Whenever Paul has been discovered, he disturbs the way we think and what we think. I want to identify three areas in which Paul's thought promises to rearrange the way we think and live; to do so I will rely on his own statement about what is lasting: faith, hope and love.

A. I begin with faith. If there is one thing that Paul is known for it is his insistence that what makes right the relation to God is faith, not our moral and religious achievements. He insisted that anyone who entrusts his or her life to God on the basis of the gospel is rightly related to God, because what God wants from us is our trust or faith. We abbreviate this insight with the phrase "justification by faith."

But Paul did more. His thought penetrated so deeply into the meaning of faith that he laid the foundation for a new understanding of what it means to be human. And this constitutes the first area in which his thought holds great promise also for us.

To see it we need to see the logic of his conviction, and it goes like this: if anyone—Jew or Greek, male or female, rich or poor—is made right with God by the same thing, faith or trust, then this must be the one answer to the one dilemma in which everyone is found. Otherwise there must be one way of salvation for Jews, another for Greeks, another for Japanese, or one for men and another for women. But if there is one salvation, then everyone's problem is the same. For Paul, the root problem of all of us is the refusal to acknowledge that God is God. Consequently, Paul discovers the solidarity of all humanity in its habit of making God over in our own image in order to serve our interests. In other words, by insisting that believing the gospel makes right everyone's relation to God, Paul has placed every human being on the same footing before God. Our shared name is Adam. In a time when we are dividing ourselves into groups according to race or gender or size of wallet, each blaming the other for its problems while regarding itself as an innocent victim, Paul's thought shows us how to think about the universally human—namely, that no one is in a privileged position before God and that everyone's relation to God can be made right in exactly the same way—by trusting God to be as good as the gospel claims. That is the first promise of Paul's thought.

B. The second promise concerns hope. Paul is future-oriented because he expects the Lord to return soon. Much of his ethical counsel flows through the filter of this expectation. Here Paul was plainly wrong. Still, there is more to his future-oriented ethics than what depends directly on his belief that the Lord's coming is near. In other words, he was wrong about the when but right about the what. So Paul's ethics invites us to base the moral life on God's future instead of on our past and present.

What concerns us here is not the specifics of Paul's ethics but the angle from which he gives moral counsel at all—the coming redemption which has merely begun in the present. Paul's moral counsel is addressed to persons who live between the "already" and the "not yet" of salvation. However great may be the redemption experienced now, it is only the appetizer; the banquet is yet to come. Paul's ethic is not for the general public. It is for people who lean into the future when their redemption will be complete; or to change the image, it is for people who are trying now to live the redeemed life ahead of time, pulling the future into the present world which is not yet redeemed. According to Paul, in Christ the ship of life has been reflagged, and now sails under the flag of hope. And therein lies Paul's second promise.

It is useful to see the alternatives to Paul's tension between the "already" and the "not yet." On the one hand, because redemption has begun already, the moral life of the Christian is shaped by the future, and that means that two kinds of ethics will not dominate. The one appeals to the way things are or natural law; the other appeals to what is useful, and so becomes utilitarian. If ethics is based squarely on the way things are, then we must do what we have always done because that is the law of nature. But for Paul, nature is the wrong standard because nature itself must be redeemed. Such a view of nature is not science; it is a religious interpretation of the fact that everything that lives must die. On the other hand, if ethics is based on what is useful, if the good and the right are what we decide to make them, then everything depends on who makes the rules. And for Paul, sinners do not make good rules, but define good and evil in ways that promote their interests. By seeing the Christian life as inaugurated redemption, Paul's ethics is really freed from the shackles of the past and open to the future and is not nearly as conservative as some of his particular advice.

One the other hand, because salvation is only begun and will be completed only when the Lord returns, Christian life is not utopian. For Paul, the only thing that keeps us from establishing a perfect world is not lack of will. Paul knows the difference between the possibility of improving life and the impossibility of perfecting it. Paul has no illusions about how saved we are or can be so long as history continues. But he has profound hope that the God who inaugurated this new possibility of the "already" will surely bring it to completion.

Those who are grasped by the promise of Paul in ethics can do as he did, and emphasize whichever point is necessary. Where there is a sense of despair because it seems nothing will ever change, we can insist on the "already," and where an overheated enthusiasm thinks that if we put our minds to it we can repeal original sin and bring in the kingdom, we can insist on the "not yet." Paul's hope requires, and enables, us to both. And that is its second promise.

C. Finally, according to Paul, the greatest thing of all is love—the passionate commitment to the good of another.

Paul sees love at the heart of the gospel. In one of his most incisive sentences he declares that God shows his love for us in the fact that while we were still sinners Christ died for us. He does not say that Christ's death shows Christ's love for God, but that the whole event of Jesus Christ happened for the sake of those who did not deserve it. It is a sheer gift given for our good, not because we are good. Nor did Christ's death cause God to love us; rather, it was God's love that sent Christ into our world where he had to die. Such love cannot be earned. It can only be received with gratitude and passed along.

Love which goes to the undeserving is the only thing that can break the chain of retribution for what is deserved, whether it is reward for the good or punishment for the bad. A system of reward and punishment is essential for all societies because people are not naturally good. So some kind of carrot and stick is essential. We need the domain of law, in which we press for a justice by which everyone gets what is deserved, no more and no less.

However, even if we could create such a world, we would not want to live in it, partly because it would be a world for achievers only, but especially because there would be no way to escape the chain of consequences of failure and wrong-doing, for in such a world there would be no place for forgiveness, no way to start over with a clean slate, no reason to help those who stumble and fall, no place for undeserved love. If we loved only those who deserved it, we would take the place of God in the judgment seat in order to determine just who deserved what from us.

Undeserved love makes it possible to say, "Nonetheless!" Undeserved love makes it possible to seek the good of another person despite what has happened. Undeserved love makes it possible to be merciful and to receive mercy. Paul understands that undeserved love is not a moral requirement we must meet but something we can hand on because we have already received it in Christ. Paul's message is not, "You must love," but "you can love because in Christ you have already been loved by God." So if we are obligated to love, it is not because we have found someone love-worthy but because we the unworthy have already been loved, and having been loved are constrained to love others as well. In a society in which everyone seems bent on making it big and making it fast for himself or herself, Paul's understanding of undeserved love, which imitates God's love, holds great promise.

6

Death and Afterlife in the New Testament

The New Testament assumes that to understand life we also must understand death and the afterlife. Yet the New Testament contains not a single chapter that summarizes the Christian view. What it says about the subject is found in a wide variety of contexts because, characteristically, the New Testament deals with death and the life after death when it talks about something else. Moreover, because the New Testament was written by many people, most of whom are unknown, and over a period of a hundred years, it says different things. Faced with such a situation, we do well to begin with a general orientation.

Introduction

Two sets of considerations will get us ready to understand what the New Testament says about death and the afterlife. The first set of considerations is that of the vocabulary and its logic. The word "death" itself is used in two senses, the literal and the metaphorical. Literally, "death" refers to the cessation of life; metaphorically, it also refers to a spiritual and moral condition. In other words, the New Testament knows as well as we do that some people are dead morally before they are dead physically. The New Testament has a different attitude, however, toward physical death. Whereas we often regard death as a neutral physiological fact, as in the antiseptic expression "She expired," the New Testament often reflects the ancient Near East view of physical death as an enemy. Never does it speak of death as a friend who releases one from pain. Consequently death and mortality are religious and theological problems: If God is the author of

PART 2: THE PRESENCE OF THE PRIOR WORD

life, why must everything that lives die? Above all, suicide is not even considered a viable option. In the New Testament, death is never in human hands; rather, it is we who are in the hands of death.

The second word we need to clarify is "immortality." Is there something in the self that is naturally immortal? The idea that the soul is naturaly immortal, deathless by definition, is at home in much of Greek thought but not in the New Testament. Not all the ancient Greeks thought that the soul was immortal, but htose who did were dualists, emphasizing the fundamental difference between what is physical, material, and mortal and what is immaterial and immortal. For them the soul is a splinter of the divine, and so is naturally immortal. The New Testament has a unique idea of immortality: The whole person will become immortal by resurrection.

So the third word we need to understand at the outset is "resurrection." In the New Testament, resurrection is not simply coming to life again. That would be resuscitation or reanimation. A resuscitated corpse will die later, but a resurrected person will never die because resurrection entails being transformed into an immortal being. According to the New Testament, we are born mortal, but our destiny is to become immortal by resurrection.

Finally, there are certain words for the place of the dead. In the Hebrew Bible, which Christians call the Old Testament, the dead go to the underworld, to Sheol, a place the Greeks called Hades. Neither Sheol nor Hades is a place of punishment. The Hebrew word for that place is Gehenna, a fiery place of torment. The English word for that is Hell. The New Testament never confuses Hades and Hell. In traditional Roman Catholic vocabulary we find the word "purgatory," the place where the dead are purified of their sins before going to heaven. The New Testament does not mention purgatory because that idea came into the Christian vocabulary much later.

These words, each with its own logic, did not simply appear; each is part of the larger complexes of ideas that have important histories. This brings us to the second set of considerations that will prepare us to look at the New Testament, that is, some historical matters.

We begin with the Greek tradition of radical dualism of the eternal, immortal soul and the mortal body made of matter. No one knows how old this dualism is in Greek thought, for it is much older than Plato, who, in the fourth century before our Era, developed it philosophically. By the beginning of Our Era the dualistic view had undergone many developments, one of which combined it with ancient Near Eastern mythology and astrology to form a widespread movement that offered salvation, a movement we call Gnosticism, from the Greek word *gnōsis*, or knowledge.[1] According to Gnostic thinking, the immortal soul is a prisoner of the mortal body. Some Gnostics coined the slogan *sōma sēma*: The *sōma* (the body) is a *sēma* (a tomb) for the soul. What makes this doubly tragic is that the body causes the soul to forget that it is a splinter of the divine. So the soul is doomed to amnesia and to one body tomb after another until it receives the true *gnōsis*, the saving knowledge, of what it really is and where it came from. Armed with this knowledge from a heavenly revealer, the soul can escape at death and return to its eternal heavenly home outside the cosmos.

The New Testament had to contend with this dualism because Christianity began with a different view of the self, one at home in the Hebrew Bible. Here the self is a besouled body, a body animated by the breath of life. The ancient Hebrews never regarded the body as the prison of the life-breath; for them the self was what we call a psychosomatic entity, God being the creator of both body and life-breath. At death a shadowy self went to Sheol, the place of the dead. This view prevailed until the second century before our Common Era when for the first time a new idea emerged—that the righeous would be resurrected. This idea solved a major theological problem created by martyrdom. It previously

---

1. Until the nineteenth century, Gnosticism was regarded as a Christian heresy that developed in the second century CE. This view reflected the fact that until then, our knowledge of it depended on the Christian theologians' polemics against its influences in the churches. Since then texts from Egypt, Iraq, and central Asia have been published; this evidence makes it quite probable that "Gnosticism" refers to a widespread religiophilosophical movement that absorbed a great variety of ideas, myths, and practices to explain a sense of alienation from the world and to offer salvation from it. Most scholars regard Gnosticism as a movement that developed alongside early Christianity; some early forms of Gnosticism appear to have influenced Christianity already in the first century. The discovery of a Gnostic library in Egypt (the Nag Hammadi Collection) in 1947 has generated wide-ranging debates over the definition, nature, originl, and influence of Gnosticism. For a useful, succinct discussion, see Elaine H. Pagels, "Gnosticism," in *Interpreter's Dictionary of the Bible Supplementary Volume*, edited by K. Crim (Nashville: Abingdon, 1976), 364-68. The Nag Hammadi texts are available in *The Nag Hammadi Library in English*, ed. James M. Robinson (New York: Harper & Row, 1977), and Bentley Layton, *The Gnostic Scriptures* (Garden City, NY: Doubleday, 1987). The most important descriptions of and quotations from early Christian opponents of gnosticism are available in Werner Foerster, *Gnosis: A Selection of Gnostic Texts*, trans. and ed. R. McL. Wilson (Oxford: Clarendon, 1972), vol. 1, *Patristic Evidence*.

was believed that those who obeyed God's will would prosper and that calamity was God's punishment for disobedience. But when it became illegal to be a practicing Jew,[2] obedient to the Law of Moses, the old theology was in a crisis because now the disobedient prospered and the obedient suffered and were killed. And so there arose the view, first clearly expressed in the book of Daniel,[3] that at the end of history, God would intervene and vidicate the righteous who had paid with their lives for being obedient, and that God would do this by resurrecting them. Not all Jews believed this, but those who did bought into a view of history known as apocalyptic.[4]

In the apocalyptic view, all history is rushing downhill toward the End, when the world as we know it, dominated by evil and death, will be replaced by the Age to Come, when everything will be made right by God. There was no single apocalyptic scenario for the End, but belief in resurrection became so important that it was retained even by those Jews who later gave up much of apocalyptic thought, the rabbis.

The point is that the Gnostic and the apocalyptist had quite different views of the self. What would have made a Gnostic shudder—the news that the soul would be reunited with the body—was exactly the basis of hope for the apocalyptist; conversely, what would have been final defeat for the apocalyptist—the unending separation of the soul from the body—was redemption for the Gnostic. To a large extent, the history of the Christian understanding of death and afterlife is the story of how

---

2. The allusion is to the effort of one of the successors of Alexander the Great, Antiochus Epiphanes IV, to prohibit the practice of Judaism in Palestine in 168 BCE. This resulted in the Maccabean Revolt, whose success three years later is celebrated in the Jewish community with the festival of Hanukkah. The story is told in 1 Maccabees, which is found in what Protestants call the Apocrypha and that Roman Catholics regard as deuterocanonical.

3. The book of Daniel, most scholars agree, was written during the Maccabean Revolt.

4. As in the case of Gnosticism (see n. 1), scholars continue to debate questions of the nature, origin, and influence of apocalyptic. The word itself comes from the Greek term *apocalypsis*, revelation. It has become clear that one must distinguish texts that claim to be apocalypses—revelations of the future—from apocalyptic ideas that are found in a wide range of literature. For a convenient survey, see Paul D. Hanson, "Apocalypticism," in *Interpreter's Dictionary of the Bible Supplementary Volume*, edited by K. Crim (Nashville: Abingdon, 1976), 28–34. For an introduction to the major Jewish apocalypses, see John J. Collins, *The Apocalyptic Imagination* (New York: Crossroad, 1984). For a discussion of the themes of apocalyptic thought, see Christopher Rowland, *The Open Heaven: A Study in Apocalyptic in Judaism and Early Christianity* (New York: Crossroad, 1982), esp. 73–189.

Christianity came to terms with both of these views. The story begins in the New Testament.

This brings us to the second historical consideration: the fundamental shift of early Christianity's center of gravity. Early Christianity began as a sect within apocalyptic Judaism, but soon became a largely gentile religion in the Greco-Roman world. The initial Christians were Jews who brought with them the apocalyptic views of death and afterlife; later, the gentile Christians—Greek, Romans, Celts—brought their dualistic ideas into the church, some of which were combined with the Jewish legacy and some of which were rejected. In the New Testament we see the beginning of this interaction.

The third historical consideration concerns the nature of the New Testament. Historically, Christianity did not come from the New Testament; rather the New Testament came from early Christianity. The New Testament did not produce Christianity the way the Book of Mormon produced Mormonism. Rather the New Testament is an anthology of twenty-seven booklets written by Christians between the years 50 and 150 CE. Each booklet was written for a particular purpose, and so takes a good deal for granted. As a result, the New Testament is not a comprehensive summary of everything early Christians believed, but a collection of writings occasioned by various needs in the churches. We should not be surprised, therefore, to find that it contains a variety of ideas about death and life after death.

Jesus

These orienting remarks have prepared us to look at what the New Testament says about our theme. Even though Jesus wrote not a single word in the New Testament, we will begin with him. Then we will examine what Paul the apostle says. After that we will look briefly at the book of Revelation, and then turn to the Gospel of John.[5]

---

5. The Gospel of John is treated separately from the Gospels of Matthew, Mark, and Luke because scholars agree that it presents a different portrait of Jesus, for it relies on traditions about his teaching that diverge significantly from those used in the other three (the Synoptic Gospels). Most scholars are convinced that the earliest Gospel is Mark, written about 70 CE, forty years after the death of Jesus. The others were written later, before 95 CE. The Letters of Paul, on the other hand, were written in the 50s CE. In other words, in the New Testament the Gospels come first even though they were written later than the Letters of Paul.

PART 2: THE PRESENCE OF THE PRIOR WORD

Jesus did not speak often about death and life after death, but what he did say shows that he was influenced by apocalyptic thought. For example, he expected that the righteous would be resurrected at the End of history.[6]

The Gospel of Mark reports that once the Sadducees, who rejected the idea of resurrection, tried to trap Jesus with a trick question (12:18–27). According to the Law of Moses, when a man died, his brother was to marry the widow. Now, the Sadduccees asked, suppose this happens repeatedly in the same family, so that finally the woman had married all seven brothers. In the resurrection, whose wife will she be? Jesus rejected the question: "When they rise from the dead, they neither marry nor are given in marriage, but are like angels in heaven" (12:25). In other words, resurrection is real transformation, not simply resuscitation. This is virtually the only thing Jesus taught about life after death. Elsewhere he simply refers to things like the coming Judgment to underscore the importance of living rightly now.

In the Gospel of Matthew, Jesus uses the phrase "kingdom of heaven." In such cases he is not talking abut the place where the blessed will go after death. Rather, "kingdom of heaven" is simply a paraphrase for "kingdom of God," since the word "heaven" is a circumlocution for God, as in our phrase, "for heaven's sake." So when Jesus speaks about having treasure in heaven (Matt 6:19, 21), he means one will have a good relation to God (see also Luke 12:13–21).

Jesus could simply allude to various parts of the apocalyptic scenario because it was not his aim to provide information about death and afterlife, but to call people to a new way of life on earth. He frequently calls attention to the coming judgment, as in some of his stories, the parables. Some of them end with a warning about people being thrown out into "outer darkness" where they will "weep and gnash their teeth" (e.g., Matt 8:12; 22:13). So, too, he urges people to deal decisively with whatever causes them to sin. "If your hand causes you to sin, cut it off; it is better for you to enter life maimed than with two hands to go to hell, to the unquenchable fire" (Mark 9:43). In all such sayings, Jesus is not providing instruction about life after death, but is referring to the future to say that the consequences of not acting rightly now are serious.

---

6. "When you give a feast, invite the poor, the maimed, the lame, the blind, and you will be blessed, because they cannot repay you. You will be repaid [i.e. by God] in the resurrection of the just" (Luke 14:13–14).

Paul

Death and life after death are much more important in the teaching of the apostle Paul. We will first see why this is the case and then see what Paul had to say about our theme.

Paul was a Jew, from Tarsus, a city in the southeast corner of modern Turkey, who went to Palestine where he joined the Pharisees,[7] for whom resurrection was a basic belief. This means that Paul believed in resurrection long before he became a Christian. Why, then, were death and the afterlife more important in his teachings than in the teachings of Jesus? Because he became a Christian when he blieved the news that a resurrection had already occurred, but in one case only—that of Jesus. Resurrection was supposed to happen for the righteous, but Jesus had been executed on a cross as a criminal. But if God resurrected him, then he was not a criminal, but a righteousn man whom God had made Lord, the heavenly regent, so to speak. The resurrection of Jesus meant even more. If resurrection marked the transition from This Age to the Age to Come, when all things would be made right, then the resurrection of Jesus implied that the time of salvation has begun. But everything seemed to be just as it was before. So how could the time of salvation have begun? Because Paul could not give up the conviction that God had raised Jesus from the dead, he, like his Christian contemporaries, reinterpreted salvation as a new right relation to God for those who believed the news of Jesus' resurrection. The complete transformation would occur when the Lord returned, at the so-called Second Coming of Christ, which would happen soon. In the meantime, believers could begin living the life of the New Age ahead of time. In other words, the death and resurrection of Jesus were the pivot on which his thinking turned. This was true of other Christians as well, but what distinguished Paul was the way he thought through the deeper and wider consequences of his conviction that God had resurrected Jesus.

One thing Paul saw clearly was that the New Age that had begun with Jesus' resurrection was decisive for the whole world. Therefore, Paul took the news of Jesus, climaxed by his death and resurrection, to the Greco-Roman world. Gentiles need not wait until the return of the Lord

---

7. The Pharisees were not priests, but laymen committed to scrupulous observance of the Torah, the Law of Moses. After the Jewish revolt against Rome in 66 to 70 CE, other groups, like the Sadducees, disappeared, but the Pharisees survived to lay the foundations of rabbinic Judaism.

Jesus before they could benefit from the salvation of the New Age. They could get in on this now by believing the gospel and by being baptized and becoming members of the church, a new international, interracial community. So Paul became the first great Christian missionary, founding congregations of believers in Asia Minor and Greece.

The Letters of Paul in the New Testament were written for these groups.[8] Paul did not write essays on topics or a book of theology. So if we want to grasp his thought, we must combine the various things he did say, risky as this may be. We cannot summarize everything he said, but we will reach for what is essential and characteristic.

Paul, being deeply influenced by the Bible, interpreted the story of Adam and Eve to mean that death entered the world as a result of Adam's disobedience or sin, and so death became the fate of humanity (Rom 5:12–21). In other words, it was sin that brought death, not the other way around. To paraphrase it, according to Paul, we do not sin because we are mortal; rather, we are mortal because of sin, not only because of what Adam did, but because ever since then everyone sins and so ratifies Adam and his consequences. This idea is so strange at first that it is useful to reflect on it a bit more.

Suppose Paul had said that we sin because we are mortal. We are more familiar with this way of thinking because it often has been said that we resist our mortality, deny our death. To assure our immortality, we devise all sorts of strategies that enhance our power over others. We exploit, suppress, and kill. In a way, we are a death-driven humanity. Paul might agree that this is a true description of what we do, but he also would insist that it is wrong as an explanation because it implies that the root problem is that we are mortal. If our mortality is the root problem, then we are innocent victims of the way we were createdd. But this implies that the real responsibility for our sin is with the Creator who made us mortal to start with. According to Genesis, God created us good, and we sinned and brought about our mortality. Human sin cannot be traced back to the Creator, but must somehow be our responsibility.

---

8. The New Testament contains thirteen letters that claim Paul as their author. Because of the differences in vocabulary, style, and content, critical scholarship has concluded that some of them were probably written in his name by his followers. Although scholars have varying judgments about the genuineness of some of the letters, all agree that seven are beyond dispute: Romans, 1 and 2 Corinthians, Galatians, Philippians, 1 Thessalonians, and Philemon.

Paul does not spend much ink explaining the origin of sin and death. His real agenda is showing how the human dilemma is overcome by God's act in Jesus Christ. How can we escape the tyranny of sin and death? By participating in Jesus' own resurrection. How can we do that? According to Paul, by being baptized because baptism makes us shareholders, so to speak, in the one event that broke the power of sin, the resurrection of Jesus (Rom 6:1–11). Paul evidently relies on the ancient view of sacraments, according to which a religious rite actually does something—imparts the life of a divine being to humans. Does this mean that baptism makes us immortal? Not at all. Paul assumed that baptized Christians would still die like everyone else. But the new Christians in Greece had problems with Paul's teaching, perhaps because he had not fully explained things before moving on.

In Thessalonika, which we call Salonika, the new Christians were distressed because some of them had died. They concluded that those who died before the coming of the Lord have forfeited their salvation. They thought that only those alive then would share in the coming salvation. Paul's First Letter to the Thessalonians corrects their thinking. When the Lord comes "the dead in Christ will rise first; then we who are alive, who are left, shall be caught up together with them in the clouds to meet the Lord in the air; and so we shall always be with the Lord" (1 Thess 4:16–17). Paul does not say where they will be with the Lord, or anything about what will happen next. He simply assures the readers that the dead Christians will not lose out.

The new Christians in Corinth seem to have had a more serious problem, one influenced by the Greek dualism we noted earlier. Some of the Corinthian Christians were saying flatly, "There is no resurrection of the dead" (1 Cor 15:12). Apparently they did not deny life after death. Rather, they rejected the resurrection because they saw the material, mortal body as the problem—a problem solved by releasing the soul from it, like liberating a bird from a cage. Paul cannot let this go unchallenged because it undercuts the gospel based on the resurrection of Jesus. In 1 Corinthians 15 we have his response.

First, he exposes the self-contradiction that the denial of resurrection implied. One the one hand, if there is no resurrection for Christians, then there was no resurrection of Christ either beause his resurrection is unique only in that it is the first. So if the Corinthians deny that Christ was resurrected, then they deny the very salvation that they prize. In fact, Paul declares, "as in Adam all die, so also in Christ shall all be made alive"

(1 Cor 15:22). On the other hand, he exposes the contradiction in what the Corinthians are doing—baptizing on behalf of the dead (v. 29). This is the only reference to such a practice, and no one knows exactly why it was done. In any case, Paul sees that if the body is not resurrected to be reunited with the soul, why bother with baptizing on behalf of the dead? Their souls are already free.

Then Paul explains what he means by the resurrection—the only passage in the New Testament that does this. He uses an analogy: We plant a seed in one form, but it comes up in another form, in another body. A grain of wheat has a brown body, but when it is planted it becomes a green one when it sprouts. So, he infers, we are buried in one kind of body but raised in another kind, what he calls a "spiritual body"—the only time he uses the phrase.

He also says why this is important: "flesh and blood [that is, our ordinary phenomenal existence] cannot inherit the kingdom of God" (v. 50). The Corinthians agreed completely. But hey had a quite different solution: Get the soul out of the body, out of flesh and blood, altogether. Paul's solution is that flesh and blood will be transformed into the spiritual body, like the grain of wheat is transformed into a green plant.

This will happen at the end, when the Lord comes: "The dead will be raised imperishable, and we shall be changed. For this perishable nature must put on the imperishable, and this mortal nature must put on immortality" (vv. 52–53). In other words, the Corinthians solved the problem of our mortality by relying on the old Greek dualistic solution of releasing the immortal soul from the body, but Paul solved it by appealing to the Jewish apocalyptic resurrection that transforms the entire psychosomatic self into an immortal being. Immortality is in store for the whole self.[9]

Finally, Paul points out what is at stake in this view—the defeat of death. Death is the ultimate enemy, the ultimate antithesis of God, the author of life. If there is no resurrection, if we must shed our bodies, if our bodies are so much unusable slag because they are material and mortal, then death has the last word after all, and God will have created

---

9. In 2 Cor 5:1–5 Paul appears to have in view a somewhat different scenario, or at least a different detail, for here he does not write of the resurrection that transforms the buried body, but of receiving a heavenly body that apparently already exists, which he calls "a house not made with hands, eternal in the heavens" (v. 1). But even here he is careful to point out that the goal is *not* for the self to be "naked" (stripped of body categorically), but to be "further clothed, so that what is mortal may be swallowed up by life" (v. 5). The passage is difficult, and interpretations vary considerably.

something that God cannot redeem. For Paul, this is completely unacceptable. So he writes that at the end, when resurrection occurs, "the last enemy to be destroyed is death" (v. 26). In other words, by resurrecting the mortal body and transforming it into an immortal spiritual one, God triumphs over death. Anything less ends in a stand-off: death being sovereign over what is mortal because of Adam's sin, God being sovereign only over souls. From Paul's angle, if that is the bottom line, then the whole event of Jesus Christ was a waste of time because as far as death is concerned, we would be exactly where we were before.

In the Letter to the Romans he goes even farther. In chapter 8 he returns to Genesis, which says that because of Adam's disobedience, the earth was cursed. Paul takes this to mean that all nature is subject to death, to what he calls "bondage to decay" (see Rom 8:20–21). He sees that everything that lives must die, and that nothing is permanent. So Paul says that creation itself will be liberated from this bondage to death. In other words, the defeat of death and decay will be total; the whole creation will be redeemed from death.

Before leaving Paul, some concluding obersvations are useful. First, although Paul writes in Greek to Greeks, he does not approach the problem of death and afterlife in Greek terms; he does not begin by analyzing the nature of the self as an unfortunate compound of body and soul. He clearly recognizes that our physical bodies are mortal, and he knows that there is an immaterial element, our spirit. But for Paul, the mortality of the body is not a fixed starting point, not a given, but the consequence of Adam and of our own ratification of Adam by our own sinning. In other words, in the last analysis, the mortality to which we are subject is not natural, but unnatural—the result of Adam. To have accepted it as natural would have implied that the human dilemma can be traced back to a jerry-built creation and an incompetent Creator.[10]

Second, what is really at stake, therefore, is the understanding of God as the creator of an originally good world, who at the End is capable of recclaiming it from its tragic history and its bondage to the consequence of sin, to death.

---

10. One theme found in many forms of Gnosticism is a repudiation of the Creator (often called the Demiurge) as a being greatly inferior to the true God, who is not responsible for the world. It is precisely this cleavage between the true God and the creator that is rejected by the Apostles' Creed: "I believe in God . . . the maker of heaven and earth."

Third, Paul shows no interest whatever in Hades or in Hell. In fact, these words never appear in his letters. Nor does Paul have any interest in exploring where the souls will be before the resurrection, just as he says not a word about life in heaven. For him, it is enough to know that the whole person will be redeemed from death and be with the Lord.

Fourth, Paul's thinking is both mythic in character and cosmic in scope. It does not describe phenomena like death or the resurrection body, but interprets these realities in language that is actually inappropriate to the subject matter because all our language is time-bound and earth-bound. Yet this is the only language that he has to talk about that which transcends time and space. Paul does not describe the undescribable, but is content to walk the boundary where he believes the decisive transformation will occur, and there to affirm what the logic of the situation requires in light of the resurrection of Jesus.

The Revelation of John

Whereas Jesus and Paul rely on certain apocalyptic ideas, there is one book in the New Testamnt that is permeated by apocalyptic themes—the Revelation of John. This book was written thirty years after Paul's death and more than sixty years after that of Jesus. No other book in the New Testament has captured the imagination of Western art or influenced the imagery of Christian hymns more than the Apocalypse of John. It apparently was written when Christians in Asia Minor were being persecuted by the state for not worshiping the divine genius of the emperor, a stance that cost them their lives. Because it was Jewish martyrdom that led to the emergence of apocalyptic theology in the first place, it is not surprising that Christian martyrdom led John the Elder to use apocalyptic to interpret the situation that now faced Christians. From this fascinating book only the elements most important for our topic will be noted, and but briefly.

The book is a series of visions that interpret John's own time and what is expected to happen shortly. Right at the outset, the resurrected Christ announces, "I died, and behold I am alive for evermore, and I have the keys of Death and Hades" (Rev 1:18). Thus those who may be killed because of their faith in Jesus are assured that death does not have the last word because Jesus has the final authority over it. As the visions of almost indescribable disaster pass before our eyes, again and again we are shown the blessed state of the martyrs. It is these visions that have provided much of the Christian imagery of life after death.

In chapter 7 John sees "a great multitude which no man could number, from every nation, from all tribes and peoples and tongues" (v. 9), standing before God's throne and before the Lamb (the resurrected Christ, who had been killed like a sacrificial lamb); these people wear white robes, the symbol of purity, and wave palm branches, the symbol of victory. Who are they?

> these are they who have come out of the great tribulation; they have washed their robes and made them white in the blood of the Lamb.
>
> Therefore are they before the throne of God,
>> and serve him day and night within his temple;
>> and he who sits upon the throne will shelter them with his presence.
>
> They shall hunger no more, neither thirst any more;
>> the sun shall not strike them, nor any scorching heat.
>
> For the Lamb in the midst of the throne will be their shepherd,
>> and he will guide them to springs of living water;
>> and God will wipe away every tear from their eyes. (vv. 14–17)

For our topic, three closely related things are distinctive in the Apocalypse of John. The first is the idea of the millennium, the 1,000 years when Christ will rule the earth as the Messiah. During this time Satan will be bound. At the beginning of the millennium the righteous will be resurrected, the Christian martyrs. After the thousand years are over Satan will be released and a final battle will take place between good and evil. Satan will be defeated and "thrown into the lake of fire and brimstone" (20:10, King James Version) to be tormented forever. Now comes the second resurrection, when all the dead will be raised and the Last Judgment will take place. The third thing is a new heaven and a new earth, to which a new Jerusalem descends (Revelation 20–21).

The reason for this scenario is clear: The first resurrection represents the vindication of the righteous martyrs. Their millennial reign is God's reward for being faithful unto death. The second resurrection is necessary to bring all the dead to the Judgment. The new heaven and earth, withs new Jerusalem, is the decisive and ultimate answer to history, with its agony and rebellion against God. No other New Testament book as this scenario.

More than any other book in the New Testament, the Apocalypse of John has given us the images of eternal bliss and eternal damnation in a fiery Hell. In a book not in the New Testament, the *Apocalypse of Peter*,[11] we get even more detailed pictures of the torment in store for sinners in Hell. Many readers find the Revelation of John to be a horrifying book; actually, its horrors have the function of providing the dark background for a profound hope.

The Gospel of John

The Gospel of John was written at about the same time as the Apocalypse of John, but by someone else in quite different circumstances. It reflects a quite different outlook as well because whereas apocalyptic theology insisted that salvation and eteral life will be given only in the future, at the End, when the Lord comes again, the Gospel of John insists that salvation and eternal life are available here and now.

Why does John insist that Jesus brings eternal life now? Because it presents Jesus as the Logos in the flesh. "Logos" has many meanings: word, reason, argument, rationale. In John it refers to the Word of God, not a book or a saying, but an eternal reality through which God created the world. This is clear in the opening lines: "In the beginning was the Word, and the Word was with God, and the Word was God. He was in the beginning with God; all things were made through him, and without him was not anything made that was made. In him was life, and the life was the light of men" (John 1:1–4). This Word "became flesh and dwelt among us," John declares (v. 14). In other words, for John, the story of Jesus is the story of what happens when the Creator becomes a man and offers real life, eternal life, to people who, it turns out, mostly refuse it. This new life means beginning all over again one's relation to the Creator by acknowledging that Jesus is the Son of God who gives life that is eternal: "For God so loved the world that he gave his only Son that whoever believes in him should not perish but have eternal life" (3:16). In other

---

11. The *Apocalypse of Peter* is available in J. K. Elliott, ed., *The Apocryphal New Testament: A Collection of Apocryphal Christian Literature in an English Translation* (Oxford: Clarendon, 1993); and in Wilhelm Schneemelcher and R. McL. Wilson, eds., *New Testament Apocrypha*, rev. ed., 2 vols. (Louisville: Westminster John Knox, 1991–92), vol. 2.

words, the Last Judgment is not in the future either, as in apocalyptic thought, but occurs whenever one says no to Jesus. Because, for John, Jesus is the Creator Logos in the flesh, saying no to Jesus has ultimate consequences that no future judgment could surpass. On the other hand, "he who believes in the Son has eternal life" (3:36). John's Jesus, therefore, declares, "Truly, truly, I say to you, he who hears my word and believes him who sent me, has eternal life; he does not come into judgment, but has passed from death to life" (5:24).

But the very next paragraph promises the traditional future resurrection.

> The hour is coming and now is, when the dead will hear the voice of the Son of God and those who hear will live . . . The hour is coming when all who are in the tomb will hear his voice and come forth, those who have done good, to the resurrection of life, and those who have done evil, to the resurrection of judgment. (5:25, 28–29)

John evidently works with a double meaning of death. The first meaning of death refers to what we call spiritual deadness. Everyone is spiritually dead until one responds positively to the Son of God, and so finds real life. The second meaning of death is lteral, and so refers to all the dead who will be reaised as in apocalyptic thought. John affirms the second meaning as part of the Christian tradtion, but is really interested in emphasizing the metaphorical meaning: Eternal life can begin now in the midst of ordinary life. Eternal life is not simply endless ordinary life, but a qualitatively different life. This life eternal is not described any more than is Paul's spiritual body. It is affirmed as a gift that one receives whenever one responds positvely to Jesus, the incarnate Word. This true life transcends physical death. The person who receives it remains mortal but will be resurrected. As Jesus says later, "For this is the will of my Father, that every one who sees the Son and believes in him should have eternal life, and I will raise him up at the last day" (6:40). It is not explained why resurrection is necessary, but we may assume that the same consideration is at work here as in Paul: What God created, the body, God will redeem.

Another idea is found only in John. During Jesus' last night with the disciples he says, "In my Father's house are many rooms; if it were not so, would I have told you that I go to prepare a place for you? And . . . I will come again and will take you to myself, that where I am you may be also" (14:2–3). In other words, Jesus promises to come to the believers in the hour of death and to take them to where he is—with God in heaven. Here, too, it is not clear why a person who has gone to the heavenly room will still need to be resurrected. In any case, this passage has become one of the most influential in Christian thought and is read regularly at funerals.

Conclusion

By no means have we looked at everything in the New Testament that concerns our topic, but enough has been seen to invite some concluding observations.

To begin with, not only does the New Testament contain a variety of ideas, but even a single author like Paul or a single book like John can say things that do not seem to fit logically. For example, Paul insists on a future resurrection, as we saw, but he also can say that if he should die, he will be with the Lord (Phil 1:23). We have seen two important reasons for this variety. On the one hand, the New Testament reflects two cultures, the Hebraic and the Hellenistic, both of which had multiple views of death and afterlife. On the other hand, because all Christians believed that Jesus was resurrected, they had to think through the consequences of this event for a whole range of questions, including beliefs about their own death and afterlife. The New Testament shows the various ways they did this in widely differing situations. More comprehensive treatments, based largely but not exclusively on the New Testament, will appear much later, when Christian theologians begin to systematize Christian beliefs.

Second, what the New Testament says about death and afterlife is always part of a much larger complex of ideas. This is inevitable because what one thinks about death and afterlife always affects what one thinks about the current life, and what makes it what it is or ought to be. Death and life are coordinate concepts. This is why, in learning what the New Testament says about death and afterlife, we found it necessary also to consider the nature of the self and the human dilemma and its resolution.

Third, many questions that people have about death and afterlife are simply ignored in the New Testament. One thinks of questions like, Will we know one another in heaven? What will the next life be like? What will happen to those who died before they heard of Christ? One passage gives a hint of an answer to this question. According to 1 Pet 3:19–20, Christ "preached to the spirits in prison, who formerly did not obey." This often is taken to mean that Christ, before his resurrection, preeached to the dead in Hades. This idea becaame part of the Apostles' Creed, in the line "He descended into hell" (i.e. to Hades). The theme became popular in medieval art.

Fourth, the New Testament writers consistently assume that each person is unique and of infinite value, even though no writer explains why this is the case. They all believe that the soul is not naturally immortal; none of them thinks that an eternal, immortal soul goes from body to body. There are two reasons for this. On the one hand, the New Testament, like the Old, believes that only God is eternal and that nothing created is coeternal. On the other hand, the idea of the transmigration of eternal souls undermines both the uniqueness of the self and the ultimate consequences of this life. What one does with this life has ultimate significance for the whole person, forever. The New Testament would accept the modern slogan "You only go around once."

Finally, it is clear that the New Testament ideas of death and afterlife are at home in a quite different world from ours. We think differently about the world, time, history, the nature of the self; and we no longer think that Hades is "below" and heaven is "above." As a result, many people no longer take literally what the New Testament says about these matters, but interpret them poetically, regarding them as powerful, and perhaps necessary, religious images that express a deep truth about the self in relation to ultimate reality, to God. In the last analysis, images are more powerful, and more important, than descriptions because images interpret and energize.

The New Testament images of death, resurrection, and eternal life have energized Western culture as well as the Christian community because they are permeated by hope in the face of pain and futility, and because they point to the Creator who does not rest until life is redeemed from death.

PART 3

The Word as Criterion

These three pieces, each in its own way, show how Scripture, when read in light of its own times and places, still functions as the criterion of Christian faithfulness—if one knows what to listen for.

The first was an address at the World Convention of the Churches of Christ, meeting in Mexico City in July, 1974. I was asked to relate the event's theme, "Emmanuel—God with Us," to Scripture. The address was published in the *Lexington Theological Quarterly* in 1975. It appears here, somewhat abbreviated and under a new title. The second address was delivered at Union Theological Seminary in Richmond, Virginia before being published in *Quarterly Review* 3 (1983). It not only develops much of what the first piece in the set asserts, but also comments on difficulties many moderns have with the Bible, precisely because is the church's norm.

My typescript does not say, unfortunately, when, where, or why the third lecture was given or who heard it. I surmise, however, that it was probably written for a consultation on evangelism, sometime between 1973 and 1979, perhaps in Nashville. If that is correct, the audience would have been leaders in the United Methodist Church's Board of Evangelism, as well as pastors keenly interested in learning what the New Testament has to say about salvation that is germane today. It is included here because, presumably, those labeled "evangelicals" are not the only ones interested in the subject. Indeed, virtually all American religion—from various fundamentalisms to assorted self-help offerings—is about salvation in some form.

7

The Penetrating Word
(Hebrews 4:12–13)

There is a danger in the topic on which I am to speak—God with us in the Scriptures. The danger is that by celebrating God's presence we will merely reassure ourselves that we are OK. But it is not at all clear that we would enjoy the presence of God as much as we think. Does it not rather appear that we are enjoying his absence? After all, an absent God leaves us to ourselves, calls no one into question, commissions no one to do his work, and lets us alone to enjoy our illusions.

So instead of reassuring ourselves, we shall think together about what happens when God comes to us through Scripture. Nor shall we praise the Bible, praiseworthy though it is, for the Bible does not ask for praise. What it asks from us is hearing, and fidelity. Nor does the Bible need our defense, our doctrines about its authority, for it is not we who save the Bible but rather it is the Bible that can save us from ourselves. Only when that occurs do we have any basis for speaking of the authority and power of the Bible.

One other preliminary remark is in order. The Bible is the book of the church, of the whole community of God's people. To be sure, the experience of hearing the Word in Scripture can also be an intensely personal event. Nonetheless when this literature became Scripture it became the canon of the church, and it is also as a community that we are to reckon with Scripture.

PART 3: THE WORD AS CRITERION

I

The text on which we shall base our reflections is Hebrews 4:12–13.

> For the word of God is living and active, sharper than any two-edged sword, piercing to the division of soul and spirit, of joints and marrow, and discerning the thoughts and intentions of the heart. And before him no creature is hidden, but all are open and laid bare to the eyes of him with whom we have to do.

What our text says about the Word of God concentrates on its function as a revealing word. Like the sharpest, double-edged sword it penetrates to the innermost recesses and lays bare what is there. That revelation occurs by the Word of God is standard belief, and that this revealing Word happens through Scriptures is fundamental as well. Yet our text surprises us because it speaks not of disclosing God, but of the unveiling of ourselves.

Our text speaks of this revealing as a piercing, a probing, a penetration that goes so deep as to be able to separate even what we find almost impossible to separate—soul and spirit. So disturbing is this text that some ancient copyists thought there must be a mistake here and changed it to speak of the separation of soul and body. But our text does not refer to the judging power of the Word of God at the moment of death, but to its probing of the living. And when we read our text in light of the question of how God is present with his church through Scripture, then the real question comes to light: How does Scripture function as the instrument of the Word that reveals the truth about ourselves? What kind of Scripture is it that can do such a thing? To be sure, the Word of God can occur through other means as well. Who has not had the Word come through to her by means of music or art or the experience of breaking bread? The capacity of the Word to occur through such means is not in question. What is before us is, How does the Word occur in the church through the medium of Scripture? What kind of Scripture do we have that allows this to happen again and again?

Biblical criticism has shown us two things about the Bible in relation to the community of faith. First, the Bible contains the literature of the community. The Bible did not produce the community, but rather the communities of faith, of Israel and the church, produced the Bible, from start to finish. In some cases the stories were handed on by word of mouth long before they were written down. The Psalms were sung in the temple before they were included in the Book of Psalms; the New

Testament contains hymns to Christ which the church sang or chanted before someone quoted them in his epistle. Likewise, the stories of Jesus were used by the church long before our Gospels appeared. At every point it is clear that the writers of the Bible used the traditions of their communities. This has two important consequences. On the one hand, the old argument between Protestants and Catholics over Scripture or tradition is largely beside the point, for much Scripture itself is written tradition. On the other hand, the Bible is not an alien authority imposed on the church. It is the literature of our own family, of our elder brothers and sisters. To be faithful to the Bible is not to be obedient to a foreign master but to keep in touch with our own forefathers, to be faithful to that part of the family who set the pace for the rest of us.

There is yet a second thing about the Bible which biblical criticism has shown us—namely, that the Bible does not simply record the traditions of the community. It is not simply a handbook which puts into writing the procedures already being followed. The Bible is really a series of critiques of the communities for which it was written. Had the faith of Israel been on target the prophets would not have denounced it. The prophets are a protest against the prevailing faith and life of Israel. In the same way, the New Testament is a critique of early Christianity. This is especially clear in Paul's letters. Had the church in Corinth, for example, been developing properly he would not have written his letters to it. The letters of Paul are nothing less (though considerably more) than a trenchant critique of his own churches. Also the Gospels put the stories and sayings of Jesus into particular patterns in order to make a point, a point designed to reshape the christologies of the churches. The same holds true for the rest of the New Testament. Much of the Bible, in other words, is a minority report, a profound and probing critique, a penetrating judgment of what the community of faith actually was and where it was going. When the writers used the community's own traditions, they did so in order to expose its distortions. The biblical writers did the same thing Martin Luther King did, for he called the American people to account by confronting us with our own Constitution, our own ideals, our own tradition of freedom. And thereby he exposed the gulf between what we said we were and the truth. In their own way, the biblical writers did the same kind of thing. They identified the fundamental traditions, and interpreted them into their communities so as to call for what the space exploration program named a "mid-course correction."

PART 3: THE WORD AS CRITERION

When the church said that this kind of writing was to be its Scripture, it canonized its profoundest critics. In other words, the church subjected itself to the judgment of these critical writings, and did so in perpetuity. For the church to live with such a Scripture, therefore, is to be continually exposed to mid-course correction. This is why we insist that the church is always in need of reformation. Scripture is not only the basis of our security, but also of our insecurity. And that is why Scripture is the appropriate instrument of the Word of God, for according to our text, the Word of God exposes us. Only by having the innermost truth about ourselves uncovered can we remain loyal to the truth of the gospel.

I want to mention briefly three areas in which this uncovering of the truth about ourselves occurs by means of Scripture, indeed, by means of what biblical criticism has shown us about the Bible.

One area has to do with our corporate memory. Europeans, Asians and Latins have not lost their memories, but most Americans have. In the USA Christians appear to have almost total amnesia. We know that persons without memories have no identity in time or place. They are lost souls. Likewise, wherever the church has no memory, it no longer knows who it is, who it belongs to, or what it is supposed to be doing. It wanders about, seeking whatever fulfillment it can find in the moment. In this situation, the Bible offers us an identity as the people of God by keeping alive the corporate memory of the church, the remembrance that we are the current generation of the people of God which stretches across time to Abraham and Sarah. It is by remembering our story that we know who we are. There are many elements in our story, but I want to speak about one which needs to be remembered.

The church has largely forgotten that it is we gentiles of all colors and continents, who, by believing in this Jewish Jesus, have become members of the people of God. According to the Epistle to the Ephesians, we multi-colored gentiles are really no people at all, but have become a people by being made members of the household of God. But we forgot our story. Had our memory not failed us repeatedly, had we remembered who we were apart from Christ and whose kin we became by faith in him, we would not have persecuted the Jews and expelled them from virtually every nation in Europe, nor could there have arisen among us an anti-Semitism that condemned six million to become fertilizer. Moreover, wherever amnesia overtakes the church and blots out its remembering that we are naturalized citizens in the people of God, we turn Christianity into a pagan Jesus-cult designed to fulfill our wants, we make of God the patron of the status quo, and turn our backs on the world of nature in order to cultivate a self-serving spirituality. But the Bible keeps reminding us that this is a perversion; it uncovers our illusions and our amnesia, and so calls us to authentic and responsible freedom of the people of God in the world. It does so by telling us a story, by reminding us that the story of Israel has become our story. And where that story is remembered, the church knows who it is, and who its Lord is.

The second area in which the Bible uncovers the truth about ourselves concerns our tragic nostalgia for the early church. How often we are exhorted to be like the early Christians! How frequently we are told, more or less, that they were the real Christians, that with them faith was real, courage strong, and prayers effective. Again and again the early Christians are held up to us as the models of what real Christians are like, and what we must strive to become. But the fact is that we are already more like the early Christians than we ought to be. The clearer becomes the picture of what was going on in Corinth or Philippi or Galatia, the more at home we feel. This is why the New Testament is as critical of us as it was of them.

The New Testament uncovers our illusions about the early church. It shows us that it is one thing to be like the early Christians, another to be what the New Testament says they should have been. The New Testament does not admire the Christians of its own time, but indicts them for the same sorts of faithlessness, the same sort of cowardice, the same sort of weak-kneed discipleship that we know all too well. There is no reason whatever for trying to restore early Christianity, nor possibility of doing so. The only book in the New Testament which looks backwards toward the good old days of the early church is the Book of Acts, and it does not do so in order to encourage a return to paradise but in order to provide a norm for the future. The New Testament does not look backward, but forward. It is time to say farewell to Christian romanticism about the early church, for we are called to the future, not to the past. By showing us the difference between an early Christian and a New Testament Christian, the Bible uncovers our misplaced nostalgia and calls us to fidelity in our own time.

The third area in which the truth about ourselves is revealed emerges when we see that the New Testament is a very pluralistic book. It is increasingly evident that the theology of Paul and John, for example, overlap at some points but are in deep conflict at others. The theology of Paul is not that of Matthew or James. There is much that all New Testament writers share, to be sure, but there are also deep disagreements as well, and they can no longer be smoothed over. The day is past when we can speak of *the* theology of the New Testament, just as today no one can find a single New Testament view of the church, of church government, or of sacraments. In other words, also here the New Testament itself has uncovered an illusion, the illusion of thinking that whereas the church we know is diverse, the New Testament shows us a single, uniform, harmonious church. This discovery, too, is saving judgment, for discovering the pluralism of the New Testament liberates the whole church today to be truly ecumenical without becoming uniform. By exposing the sectarianism of all our particularities, including our various minimum demands for Christian unity, the New Testament's own diversity calls us forward to a church which is ecumenical precisely because it is pluralistic.

In these three areas—the recovery of identity through corporate memory, the exposure of our romanticism about early Christianity, and radical pluralism of the New Testament—Scripture uncovers the truth about ourselves. Thereby the Word of God penetrates to the heart of our illusions and makes us free.

II

But our topic has to do with God's presence in Scripture. What does this uncovering of the truth about ourselves tell us about God's presence with his church by means of such a Scripture? Moreover, we live in a time when for many persons the word "God" has become empty, and seems to refer to no reality in particular. Perhaps Paul Tillich was right when he once remarked that we may be living in the time of the silence of God, when God seems to have withdrawn himself. In such a time, when we find it difficult to speak of God at all, can our text help us recover the reality of God? I believe it can.

First of all, our text implies that the character of God is disclosed by how he meets us. That is nothing less than a radical and revolutionary understanding of what the word God means. Our text does not permit us to think that the God who meets us in Scripture is the God we expect, because the God we expect to find there is the God we assume we know, the God whom we try to manage, the God who again and again turns out to be the creation of our own minds or the one who guarantees the values of our class or race or sex. Such a god is created by the thoughts and intentions of the heart, as our text implies. He stands for what we already are or want to be. Such a God is the enlarged image of ourselves. Are not women telling us that there is a correlation between our image of God and our male superiority? Are not the oppressed of the earth accusing us because our image of God supports our economic exploitation of the poor and the weak? So long as we expect to meet any God who is but the counterpart to ourselves, we are not prepared for what can happen when we meet the real God. You see, the God who makes himself present in the unveiling of ourselves first of all disassociates himself from the god we bring to the text. The God we bring to the text does not penetrate us, does not uncover us, because he does not stand over against us. He is really our shadow, our guardian angel, our heavenly double. But the God of whom the text speaks has an identity of his own, and a freedom of his own, by which he uncovers our illusions and our idolatry. Whenever the unpleasant truth about ourselves is uncovered, there this God is present. East of Eden, where we all are living with the sons of Cain, the real God meets us first of all in his otherness, his strangeness, his judgment, in the uncovering of the truth about ourselves.

Let me restate the point. What Scripture uncovers about us is not scientific truth about the origin of the species called man, but the moral truth about the human heart and its illusions about itself. The illusions about ourselves always carry with them illusions about what is real and reliable; that is, illusions about ourselves are part of illusions about God. But the experience of seeing illusions melted away, especially illusions about God, is a sign that God himself is present. We know that God loves us because he does not leave us in our illusions. It is of course true that God's presence is not limited to the experience of judgment. But if there is no judgment in the experience, or if it is muted so as to be virtually gone, it is not the God of the Bible who is present but some other thing we call God. More important, in our time especially, recovering the sense of the reality of God depends far less on our experience of what warms the heart than on the experience of being uncovered, for there is too much blood on our hands to find the real God only in the experiences we enjoy. And so the experience of being uncovered by Scripture mediates to us the presence of the living God who is the Holy One in our midst.

In the second place, our text apparently speaks of God as the one to whom we are accountable, though the language is hard to translate precisely. In any case, Scripture never loses sight of the accountability of humankind. This accountability is infinitely richer in meaning than a childish conclusion that we are on perpetual parole. It rather signifies the dignity of man, the irradicable human capacity to be and to do, and to be responsible for what we are and achieve. God takes us more seriously than we take ourselves, for we are always hiding ourselves in the mass of humanity, or hiding the mass itself in impersonal forces like economic factors or the mentality of the times. But we cannot escape our responsibility so easily, at least not if we keep reading the Scripture.

Whenever we excuse ourselves from responsibility for the dehumanizing poverty, disease and exploitation of man by man, Scripture uncovers our conscience by showing that we are Cain, asking that self-indicting question, "Am I my brother's keeper?" Whenever the church admires itself, Scripture uncovers its responsibility for having become another Ephesus, whose first love has grown cold. In other words, the God who becomes present in Scripture makes us responsible and thereby gives us our dignity. It is not who we are by nature that gives us our human dignity, but who we are when we are made accountable by the presence of God that makes us truly human.

But for what are we accountable? Our text does not spell it out, but assumes it. In the third place, then, we are accountable for our humanness, a humanness which we find in the company of Jesus. In other words, we are accountable for our discipleship. According to the New Testament, God's purpose is manifest in Jesus Christ, who gave it flesh and made it deed. We cannot read the Scripture without having it brought home to us that committing ourselves to Jesus means committing ourselves to what he was about. Scripture, in other words, pulls us forward into mission.

The time of so-called "foreign missions" may be over, for our younger brothers and sisters are telling us Westerners, "Missionary, go home!" But the day of mission is always at hand for the whole church. We cannot read the Scripture without hearing about this Jesus who made persons human in the setting where he found them. When the truth about God comes alive, when the truth of our accountability to him comes home to us, then we also know who our brothers are and what our tasks must be. The God who comes to us through Scripture calls us to his Christ. And where is this Christ to be found? Wherever there is human pain that calls for healing, wherever a human person is crying out for freedom and dignity.

Let us not pervert Scripture by hiding behind a literalism which says that because Jesus did not reform the taxation system in Palestine, nor call for the Romans to withdraw their troops, nor demand emancipation for slaves, therefore we need not do such things either. Whoever thinks this way is Adam, using Scripture as his fig leaf to conceal his guilt, to hide his identity and to justify the status quo. It is a phoney discipleship that appeals to what Jesus did not do in his time and place in order to keep things as they are in ours. But the Scripture speaks of the commitment of God to redeem his creation from death, to redeem his creatures from their mutual self-destruction, to bring his Kingdom upon the earth so that his will shall be done here as it is in heaven. In other words, the God who comes to us in Scripture is the God who has committed himself to overcoming the moral gulf between reality in his presence and reality among mankind, who has pledged himself to make the world the image of heaven. The God who comes to us in Scripture dignifies man by making him accountable for his partnership in that project, and thereby lifts our eyes to the horizon of God's future.

How then is God present to the church in her own Scripture? By uncovering the truth about ourselves he points to the truth about himself, and calls us to perpetual reformation so that we might share in God's own mission of liberating the world from bondage to every kind of death which robs mankind of life. Whoever meets this God through Scripture knows who God is, knows who he himself is, knows what the church is to be about and who are the brother and sister. When Scripture mediates the presence of God we are not called backward to a golden age that never was, but forward to the frontier of the Kingdom where God is real. It is time to get the story straight, to make it our own again, and it is time to move forward toward freedom. When that happens, we will know indeed how God is present among us through Scripture.

8

Scripture and Canon

The title of this essay is deliberate, even though at first glance one of those terms appears to be redundant, like "each and every." Scripture and canon sound like two words for the same thing, like car and automobile. Actually, of course, car and automobile are to be distinguished, although in common parlance we use them interchangeably. So too with regard to Scripture and canon. It is useful to see that each word has its own range of associations and meanings. In the word Scripture we recognize the Latin term *scriptura*, that which is written, the writings. The New Testament uses the Greek *hē graphē* or the plural *hai graphai* to express the same idea, but normally we translate the Greek as "scripture," not simply "writings," in order to indicate which writings are being mentioned—the writings which are deemed special, sacred or holy, inspired, revealed. Canon, on the other hand, is English for *kanōn*, the Greek word for measuring rod, norm, or standard. When we want to connote the intrinsic special quality of a body of writings we use the word Scripture or Scriptures, but when we want to connote their standing in the community we use the word canon. Canon suggests the formal, juridical standing which Scripture does not.

This distinction locates more precisely the subject-matter of this essay: the place of the canon in the life of the church. Distinguishing Scripture from canon does not mean abandoning the one for the other. Indeed, because the word *canon* refers to a closed collection, two things at least are clear. First, this literature was acknowledged to be Scripture before it became canon; second, the canon retains its role in the church primarily because it continues to be Scripture: special writings which have a special capacity to be the vehicle for what we confess is the Word of the Lord. No doctrine of biblical authority generates this experience of this Word. Canonicity is the formal and official acknowledgment by the community that these writings are indeed Scripture. This means that the Bible's standing in the church depends on the church's experience of it as Scripture. Where the Bible ceases to function as Scripture, as special, it ceases to be the canon and becomes instead a resource book on a shelf of great religious classics.

Conversely, the Bible can be experienced as Scripture and yet fall short of being the canon. One of the tasks before us is the rehabilitation of the Scripture as the canon of the church, as the acknowledged norm to which the community knows itself to be accountable, and with which it must come to terms. It is this task that makes the distinction between Scripture and canon significant.

Now if "canon" refers to the Bible as that body of literature with which the community must come to terms, and if "Scripture" refers to the Bible as that body of literature through which one experiences the word so intensely, so intimately, so powerfully that one confesses it to be the Word of the Lord; and if the latter is necessary for the former, then theological education for the church faces a formidable task indeed. For we are tempted by two shortcuts which at first appear to be quite different but which turn out to be quite similar.

On the one hand, our work is proceeding at a time of a strong and growing interest in what is commonly called "spirituality." Protestants have learned to use the Catholic language of formation: the shaping of the whole person into a more fit servant of the gospel. Spirituality is a great attraction today for seminars, clinics, retreats, and the like. Surely this strong interest in spirituality has many roots, but equally sure is the fact that it bespeaks a wide and deep hunger for what used to be called vital, personal religion. It is not rare for pastors to reflect rather caustically on the spiritual aridness of their theological education, on its intellectualism or lack of attention to their own personal growth in faith, or in deepening the capacity to pray. As far as the current scene is concerned, the more we have students in theological schools who themselves are looking and exploring and ascertaining whether the "Christian thing" is really for them, the more strain is placed on the seminary whose ethos is more that of a school for educating the committed than of a church for nurturing the seekers. Some schools feel themselves infiltrated by charismatics and evangelicals, and faculties sometimes reassure one another that in our shop, at least, such students pose no real problem—yet.

The surge of interest in spirituality impinges on our topic in a very interesting way, for if there is one thing that seems to characterize the use of the Bible in the many forms of spirituality it is the almost complete disregard of the Bible as it is taught in the classroom. What is encouraged is the experience with the Bible as Scripture, as the means for deepening ones spirituality directly, uncluttered by any critical judgments. It is true, to be sure, that for many persons, matters of sources, dates, authorship, literary integrity, and the like, allow one to make sense of a baffling book. It is also true that for many others, the Bible comes alive only when these matters are ignored as they listen for what the Lord is saying to them or to us. What seems to be missing, and sorely needed, is an interpretive scheme, a hermeneutic, a theology of exegesis which makes clear the relation between the historical explanation and spiritual or moral appropriation. Faculties are generally much more adept at breaking up the hardpan clay of fundamentalism than they are in clarifying the relation between explanation and appropriation. What we usually say is that there is no recipe, no set of procedures for moving from one to the other. True enough. But that answer alone is no longer satisfactory; further reflection is in order.

To speak of explanation in biblical study is to speak of historical criticism, mostly done by experts. To speak of appropriation and interpretation is to speak of what is done mostly by amateurs, which is not simply a word for laity. So the question becomes, "If it is the amateur scholar who interprets for the church in accord with his or her appropriation of the text, what is the role of the experts' explanation in this process?" In explanation we try to account for phenomena in the text, and in historical explanation we do so by appealing to antecedents, to earlier sources, borrowed ideas, reused traditions, motifs, and the like. For decades experts have had an unquenchable thirst for antecedents and parallels, and they have succeeded remarkably in anchoring the biblical anthology in the cultures of antiquity. The experts have also succeeded in making it difficult to talk with one another. A specialist in the Synoptics is often reluctant to be caught with his hand in the Gospel of John. Experts in Jewish backgrounds concentrate on the Septuagint, or the Targums, or in obscure apocalyptic texts, or on Samaritans and Essenes. Experts in premonarchic Israel sense that they are strangers and sojourners in the post-Exile literature. In no way do I want to belittle the erudition that this expertise, developed across lifetimes, represents. Even though one sometimes has the impression that the flour is being ground again, on the whole this unprecedented examination of every aspect of the Bible has brought to light an enormous amount of information and considerable body of insight. But no one can master the field anymore. As a result even the experts are amateurs outside their narrow plots. It is little wonder that the student or the pastor is bewildered by this entire explanatory process and its apparatus.

There is another consequence of this massive, explanatory work which makes bridging explanation and appropriation difficult: namely, that historical explanation, in effect, rearranges the Bible. Books are disassembled and reconstructed and put into different sequence, so that we can trace the historical development. The historical student of Paul reads him as a moving target who appears with I Thessalonians and disappears with Romans. Raymond Brown's recent book, *The Community of the Beloved Disciple,* disassembles the Johannine corpus and rearranges the material in order to write the history of a tradition. In both Old and New Testaments we study texts that do not even exist but that must be inferred, namely, the Yahwist and Q. So powerful is this rearranging done for the sake of reconstructing the past accurately that a by-product has emerged as well—a sense of intimidation on the part of the amateur. Instead of giving entry to the text, our sophisticated methods of explaining the data create the impression that unless all methods are mastered and orchestrated properly the Bible is more forbidding than ever. The message that seems to come through to student, pastor, ethicist, theologian, counselor is this: do it right or leave it alone.

Given these developments, it is little wonder that persons interested in spirituality find it virtually impossible to link up their concern with explanatory biblical study, and so simply abandon it when they pursue what they regard as really important anyway—direct, spiritual appropriation.

On the other hand, there is another shortcut which, as noted above, turns out to be virtually the same, namely, the rising disregard of the historically oriented explanatory process for the sake of various ahistorical explanatory efforts, whether some form of literary criticism or what goes under the banner of "structuralism." Instead of reading narratives in order to learn what happend or to determine how much the narrative can tell us about what happened, the interest is in the narrative-world created by the storyteller, whether the story refers to an actual event or not. To encounter that created world of meaning, to enter it appreciatively, is goal enough. For these critics the goal is to understand precisely how language works, to arrive at a kind of analytical X-ray of the text as a text, to see it as a whole, as a work of art, and not as a quarry for either facts or dogma. Repeatedly the ahistorical mode of inquiry reminds us that so much biblical study has been preoccupied, perhaps excessively, with historical questions, with genetic relationships so that other important, useful questions have been ignored. Interestingly enough, the newer ahistorical modes can be more effective temptations away from historically oriented explanation precisely because they too operate in the explanatory mode. They too account for phenomena in the text, promise to help readers understand it and appreciate it, but do so in another mode. Indeed, whereas people who bypass historical study for the sake of spirituality can sometimes be accused of anti-intellectualism, persons who press for the ahistorical modes are highly sophisticated and much of the work has developed its own jargon, its own gurus, its own group of cognoscenti. Moreover, part of the appeal is the critique of all previous scholarship as having been concerned with the wrong questions anyway. Even if on closer examination there is considerable diversity among the participants, there is a kind of messianism in this movement away from the historical. But the point I want to make is this: that the more this kind of biblical study, suggestive and insightful though it can be, turns away from history, the more it approaches charismatic exegesis, because what matters is the transaction between the individual reader and the text. Here too, there is a quest for meaning which does not rely on understanding the text in its historic embeddedness. What matters is having one's spiritual and aesthetic and moral sense enlivened. In this mode of study, the Bible can be Scripture, but need not be canon because continuity with the historical community is irrelevant. The community that matters is the community of discourse which consists of those who read texts in the same way.

I said that theological education faces a formidable task. It is to find a way to continue the historical explanatory process in such a way as to make it more fruitful in the life of the church. This requires not repudiating the current literary, ahistorical approaches but rather incorporating them—a possibility that cannot be explored here. It must suffice to affirm that the Bible is Scripture so that it can become again the canon of the community—that anthology with which the church must come to terms again and again. And here we reach the footing on which this lecture stands—the inseparability of canon and community.

What I am proposing is that biblical scholarship can help the church move forward toward recovering the canonicity of its Scripture by following through on what historical explanation has allowed us to see, and that theological scholarship can help the church develop a more ample understanding of canon. I want to say a word about each possibility. What historical study of the Bible has allowed us to see is that the relation between canon and community does not need to be created but recognized and released. Through historical-critical study of the Bible it has become abundantly clear that the Bible is so involved in the communities of faith that it cannot be isolated from them. The materials behind the present texts were handed on in the communities. When the books of the Bible were written they came into existence in response to the needs of the community. The books were edited and compiled into the texts we have in order to make the texts serviceable for synagogue and church. The manuscripts we have were prepared for community use, and both the formation of the canon and its actual shape is the work of communities. Even if one allows for diversity in the case of the Old Testament, the basic point remains the same. What we know as the canon is inextricably involved in the life of the community at virtually every point until modern times. In short, historical criticism has made it abundantly clear that we would not have the Bible we have without the church.

What is not so clear, however, is whether we can have the church without the canon. I am persuaded that we cannot. Societies and groups and projects concerned with religion we can have in abundance without canon. Religious experiences, even meaningful ones, and access to truths we can have without having the canon, but without canon we are not church.

Now this claim deserves to be considered a bit more. It is of course true that the church existed without the New Testament or the texts which some of its books incorporated, but even then the church used the Scripture of the synagogue. Even if the synagogue canon was not yet closed by the Jewish community, most of the books of the New Testament used the synagogue Scripture as an authoritative text. It is also true that the whole church never agreed on what books constitute the Old Testament. In any case, even if there is some variation in what constitutes the Old Testament, today each church has a canon, a closed collection. There is no way to undo this, to return to a first-century situation *de jure*. In principle, to be sure, any church can change the content of its canon. But actually this is no longer possible. Even sharply defined groups like Christian Scientists and the Latter-day Saints have provided themselves with canonical supplements rather than change the inherited canon, the former being the key to the Scriptures and the latter a parallel canon. As the articles of faith printed on a card left by a Mormon missionary put it, "we believe the Bible to be the word of God as far as it is translated correctly. We also believe the book of Mormon to be the word of God." (Evidently there is no ambivalence about that translation.) The same bondedness of church and canon is reflected when liberal groups attend also to the writings of other religions: the more these other texts are valued, the less concern there is to be specifically and avowedly part of the traditional Christian church.

A more adequate view of canon helps the church understand itself in a truly historical way. When the Bible is canon it links one specific historical community to another and the whole church at a given time to its predecessors reaching back as far as Abraham and Sarah. By sharing this canon, we, who may be Anglo-Saxons or Asians, or Africans or Melanesians, appropriate a common funding history, a common vocabulary and imagery, common expectations and values. The more one senses the fuller scope of what is entailed in the relation of canon and community, the more aware one becomes of the impoverishment that marks much of the church's use of the Bible as mere Scripture—as a body of important and special texts whose standing nonetheless falls short of what a more ample canonicity can entail. Even the church's appeal to the Bible as the final warrant for doctrines falls short, for it tends to constrict the Bible's role to that of providing right beliefs and ideas. For much of the church the chief value of the Bible is to provide revealed ideas or authorized morals. Proof-texting abounds among liberals no less than among conservatives. Inevitably, placing the primary emphasis on right ideas or proper morals leads to the idea that the true church consists of the right-minded or the morally superior. It is not hard to see why this is the case: the Bible is being used as a series of warrants, a use that is inevitably supportive because it is selective.

The two moves away from historical-critical study provide no real antidote for this, because a direct appropriation of Scripture for spirituality is even more selective and it nurtures a sense of community grounded in similar religious experiences. That is, it produces a sense of the church which is finally pietistic. An aesthetic reading of Scripture nurtures a sense of community which is essentially gnostic, an intellectually suggestive experience possible for those who have been initiated into a precise method and a rather arcane vocabulary available to the elite. This approach does not link todays community with its predecessors apart from the forebears in the history of research.

PART 3: THE WORD AS CRITERION

What is called for is an approach to the Bible which does not forfeit its role as Scripture but which goes beyond so that it becomes a canon of the community in a more ample way, in a way that builds on what historical study has disclosed about it. One way to achieve this is by overcoming the selective use of the Bible in worship, whether as the basis for doctrine, morals, inspiration, or imaginative insights. Even though preaching is an essential aspect of worship I shall not repeat what I published in *The Bible in the Pulpit*. It is rather the role of the Bible at the lectern that is in view just now.

Even if the Bible is read every Sunday, the fact is that the *way* it is read virtually precludes the more adequate canonicity of the Bible in the community. Today the only contact most Christians have with the Bible occurs on Sunday morning. This is what makes the use of the Bible in the church and in worship so important and often so tragic. One can attend every service for years and never encounter more than a series of fragments. If a lectionary is not used, one Sunday's reading is from Genesis, the next from Philippians, the third from Amos, and so on. The Bible is read as if it were a scrapbook, an assortment of useful passages with no design, no plot, no overarching saga or drama. Even if a lectionary is used, the three-year cycles seldom add up to sustained attention to any given book as a whole. With or without a lectionary, the Bible is fragmented and the congregation deprived of a sustained experience with its canon.

The consequences are made all the worse by the general ignorance of the Bible in the community and by the way it is usually read at the lectern. One may doubt whether any literature is read in public the way the Bible is read in most cases. I refer not only to the holy tonie of voice, the mumbling of phrases, and mispronunciation of words, and the like. I refer to the fact that what is read is torn from the context and read as if it were a telephone number, intelligible in itself without any before or after. Now to be sure, announcing chapter and verse is a stylized way of announcing the context, and in some cases an invitation to read along. But if the hearers do not know their way around the Bible, it communicates nothing at all; better to have the page number. To be sure, a parable or Psalm can stand alone; but sections of narratives or parts of extended arguments, as in the Epistles, have a setting in the text. A few sentences which give the setting make hearing the lection much more meaningful because the hearer gets the sense of an intelligible whole. What we usually get instead are pious words like "Hear the words of the Lord as it is written . . . ," followed by, "May God bless this reading to our understanding"—little short of daring God to overcome what just happened. This treatment of the Bible violates what we believe and know the Bible to be, for it simply displays a fragment of a relic as if it were the shinbone of an apostle. The Bible cannot function as the canonical companion of the community when it is mistreated this way in worship.

What is needed is a sustained encounter with the entire Bible, begats and all. This requires us to surround the public hearing of the whole canon with a familiarization of it in the classroom. Only then will the church be able to come to terms with it as its canon. The coming to terms with the canon entails more than studying those passages which can easily serve as warrants for things we already believe and for a course of action to which we are already committed—little more than extended proof-texting. Such carefully screened, selective attention to the canon is as reprehensible in the hands of liberals as it is in the hands of conservatives. Coming to terms with the canon entails a serious encounter with the Bible as it actually is, not with the Bible as we wish it were.

Only if the community of faith deals with all of its canon can it come to an adequate understanding of what it is and what it has been. Only such an understanding allows the community to deal with both its identity and its history in a responsible way. Coming to terms with the Bible also entails allowing our perceptions and convictions to be challenged by the canon, a process in which we know ourselves accountable to it. The sheer diversity of the Bible, as well as its particular contents, elicits from the community reflection on fundamental questions because while the whole Bible is equally canonical it is not all equally binding for faith and action. By distinguishing what is authoritative for our own faith and life from what is no longer mandatory, the community comes to maturity.

Three current issues make this point concrete. One is the awareness that in many ways the Bible is a patriarchal book, and that at certain points the translations make the matter even worse. Coming to terms with this aspect of the canon should be the occasion for the community of faith to think through fundamental matters, not simply to tinker with the translations in order to make them more accurate or palatable, and certainly not simply to ventilate outrage. Another issue concerns the manifest antipathy toward the Jewish communiy expressed in important parts of the New Testament. Rather than issue an expurgated edition from which these passages are removed, as was done for the Fourth Gospel some years ago, it is better to leave the text as it is and to declare that these passages reveal how our forebears reacted to polarized situations and that their reactions are just that—theirs not ours, and reactions not revelations. Thereby the community today can mature in its identity and take responsibility for its past. A third issue concerns the New Testament disinterest in matters of public policy such as the abusive Roman system of taxation, police brutality, the imperial system itself, and slavery. Nowhere does the New Testament call upon Christians to ameliorate these things, let alone restructure society. To hide behind the silence of the New Testament is as irresponsible a use of the canon as it is to make John a liberation theologian or Jesus a Jewish freedom fighter. Both ways proceed on the basis that the Bible must say what we want it to say and need for it to say. Neither claims the freedom to let the past, including the canon rooted in the past, be what it actually was. Relating to the Bible as canon does not require the community to perpetuate the past but does require it to come to terms with its past as a necessary and unavoidable aspect of mature faithfulness today. Having this anthology as our canon does not settle questions but raises them in perpetuity.

We can now return to the port of entry for these remarks—namely, the role of scholarly explanation for interpretation in the community. In the first place, the process sketched is indeed a community process, one in which there is conversation and argument, not simply propaganda for points of view. That conversation in turn rests on the fact that no one is only right and that no one is immune from correction. The difference between the expert and the amateur is relativized when both are members of this community, when each is prepared to learn from the other. Moreover, the pastor's work includes developing the emotional maturity and stability which such a conversation assumes and requires. Furthermore, just as there is no risk-free historical explanation, so there is no risk-free interpretation. In interpretation we rely as much on justification by faith as we do in redemption. Finally, this view of the canon rests solidly on the historical-critical method which has exposed the ways in which the canon is rooted in the multiple cultures in which it was written. The same method has made us aware that we ourselves are no less rooted in our own culture, with its prejudices and blind spots, than the prophets of Israel or the apostles of the church. Consequently the community of faith has a stake in the ongoing health and vitality of the historical-critical study of the Bible and the history of its interpretation. Far from being the great danger to the church and its canon, historical criticism is the essential method if the church wants to understand itself as a historical community with a historical canon bearing witness to a historical faith.

9

The Gospel's Promise of Salvation

The Gospel's promise of salvation must make its way in the open market where other modes of salvation are being offered. This has been the case from the start, even if it was obscured for a number of centuries by so-called Christian civilization. Today, however, the gospel's promise of salvation must not only compete with other promises but defend itself against attack because some of these alternatives are deliberately anti-Christian and hence anti-Jewish as well. This is because the understanding of God and of the human condition as grounded in the Bible is regarded as a part of the problem. At least since the French Revolution, there has been a growing and steady stream of thought which has contended that the real salvation of humanity cannot coexist with the God of the Bible and of Christianity. This is the case not only with regard to thinkers like Marx and Nietzsche who addressed the issue head on, but also for those who do not make the matter explicit. More important, various aspects of neo-paganism have been around long enough that they can no longer be regarded as the ideas of a few alienated intellectuals; to a remarkable degree these ideas have seeped into both popular mind and the common unconscious. Consequently the gospel's promise for salvation loses its potency if the promise is not clarified vis-à-vis these repudiations. The young evangelical theologian at Westmont College, Ray Anderson, put it well: "Incoherence has no power of confrontation, and thus carries with it neither an ultimate demand upon us nor an immediate possibility for the communication of the truth."[1] In other words, we must become theologians if we are to proclaim a promise that has power to save.

1. Ray S. Anderson, *Historical Transcendance and the Reality of God: A Christological*

But what kind of theologians? There are three major options being pursued today. One insists that the only way to maintain the integrity and power of the promise is to repeat in a direct, straightforward way the words, beliefs, and horizons of the Bible, recognizing that this carries with it the demand to defend the Bible itself as a repository of revealed information and ideas. In effect this point of view argues that the Bible is credible if Jonah is edible. This often produces a siege mentality, which makes it difficult to convey the gospel as a promise which evokes joy and freedom. Instead, salvation is an island of security.

A second mode of response is characterized by an ongoing adjustment to the culture. Liberal Protestantism has been characterized as a series of fire sales in which the merchandise was offered at evermore reduced prices in the hope of staying in business. By now there's not much stock on the shelves. The gospel's promise appears to be a paraphrase of what is available elsewhere, and without a church budget to support.

The third option is much more difficult, but is the only way I find viable. This is an attempt to grasp afresh the biblical and classical Christian theological insights and to discover their radicality in our day in a way that is analogous to their original radicality. This cannot be mere repetition and reassertion, nor is it sheer accommodation to the modern mind, whatever that is. It rather does again what was done by the New Testament writers—bring the givenness of the tradition, that is the New Testament, into confrontation with the present in order to create a crucible in which the power of the tradition is discovered afresh. That in any case is what I hope to do as we reflect on certain motifs in Paul's letter to the Romans. Concretely, I want to probe and reflect on the import of Rom 10:1–17.

I

This passage is so complex and so sophisticated that we owe it to Paul and to ourselves to get our bearings first. To begin with, at first glance the theme of salvation emerges here almost as a digression, because Paul's real problem in Romans 9, 10, and 11 is the refusal of the Jews to acknowledge Jesus as the Messiah. That problem both begins and ends our passage. We would not go wrong if we said that it was the Jews' refusal

---

Critique (Grand Rapids: Eerdmans, 1975), 103.

to be evangelized that forced Paul to reflect more deeply on the gospel's promise of salvation.

In the next place, Paul is wrestling with his problem in conversation with scripture. It was the interpretation of the scripture which prevented the Jews from accepting the gospel. Therefore, it was in scripture that Paul had to find the answer. The entire exposition of the gospel's promise of salvation here is governed by the phrasing of Old Testament lines that Paul changes, appropriates, and interprets in a way that reminds us of the Dead Sea Scrolls.

More important, in the third place, is recognizing that here, confession with the mouth that Jesus is Lord and believing with the heart that God raised him from the dead, is a single indivisible act. This means that the two statements in v. 10 interpret one another—namely, "With the heart one believes for righteousness, and with the mouth one confesses for salvation." Consequently righteousness and salvation are two sides of the same coin. Salvation has to do with righteousness. In other words, the gospel's promise of salvation is first of all the promise of righteousness, not a promise for improving our personality or getting rid of personal sins. Those are dealt with as part of something more important—righteousness. But what is righteousness, as Paul understands it?

Obviously, this righteousness comes from God. It is God's righteousness. But what is its scope and focus? Slightly over a decade ago, Ernst Käsemann began a rather intense debate with Bultmann over the meaning of the phrase, "God's righteousness," and argued that it was not only grounded in the Old Testament but that in some cases it does not refer primarily to a right relation which God grants the individual who believes, but that it refers to God's sovereignty over a restored creation. In these cases its scope is cosmic, not oriented to the individual heart. I am persuaded that Käsemann is on the right track. This means that the old debates over whether the righteousness from God is imputed or imparted, whether God treats the sinner as if one were righteous even though one is not, or whether God makes the sinner righteous, are off-base. Interestingly, the resulting debate among Lutheran exegetes in Germany has been picked up by Latin American liberation theologians. Käsemann's influence is clear and acknowledged in José Miranda's highly important book *Marx and the Bible*. Thus critical exegesis need not be a sterile exercise in antiquity's texts; it can have explosive consequences for life today. Preaching that is grounded in exegesis may be the real key to evangelism today, as always.

What then does Paul mean by God's righteousness? The word "righteousness" is one translation of the Greek word *dikaiosynē*, which can also be translated as justice, from the Latin *justitia*. English has no verb for "make righteous"—we can't get by with "righteousify"—so we switch to the Latin and say justify. But thereby we land in some problems. For one thing, justify usually means giving adequate reasons for doing something. When we use it of ourselves, it takes on the meaning of giving excuses. "He's simply trying to justify himself." Now these usages of justify reinforce the idea that Paul's meanings of justification, of making righteous, of righteousness, are oriented primarily toward the individual.

The theologians of liberation, however, have rediscovered Paul—that is they have learned that the righteousness of God is a riche, dynamic, indeed revolutionary concept. In their situation they may over-emphasize this aspect, but we status-quo Christians are hardly in a position to accuse them of reflecting their biases. If they are politicizing the gospel, we have privatized it so long that we scarcely can think in any other categories.

Paul's understanding of righteousness is grounded in the Old Testament and shaped by apocalyptic. In the Old Testament that is right which accords with the norm. There is an echo of this in our phrase "the upright person." Because God is the final norm of what is right, on one level the righteousness of God means God's own righteousness, God's own moral integrity. On another level, God's righteousness cannot be restricted to his internal integrity, but must be extended to his creation. An internally righteous creator is committed to making right the distorted creation. God's righteousness is manifest only when all things are right, that is in right relation to God and to one another. The verb "to make right," which we translate "justify," therefore should be translated "rectify." Actually there is one instance when we actually use justify in this sense—the electric typewriter which justifies the margin. It does not supply adequate reasons for the margin, it aligns it. The machine makes it right, makes the ragged endings straight.

That is what justification is all about—the rectification of human life. The focus of righteousness is the relationship to the norm, It has to do with the relationship between persons, between persons and the world, between groups, and the relation of the self to the self, and the self to its Creator. The more distorted the human condition, the greater the demand on internal rectitude of God to align the human life. The greater the resistance to alignment, the more dramatic the rectification will turn out to be.

It is in light of these fundamental meanings that we must read the promise of the gospel as Paul developed it in the Letter to the Romans. When we do, important things become clear. Let me identify a few of the major ones. First, the reason Paul describes at considerable length and depth the human situation in Romans 1–3 is to clarify what it is that needs to be rectified and why. It is indeed the case that Paul does not mention things which we would include, such as slavery, and that he includes things which we might omit, such as homosexual acts. The extent to which the content of Paul's portrait of the Gentile world is shaped by Jewish literature and tradition need not detain us. It is sufficient to recognize that the discussion begins with the claim that God's wrath is disclosed against *all* human impiety and unrighteousness (Rom 1:8).

Second, over against this, the righteousness of God is unveiled in the gospel. Decisive is the fact that for Paul the gospel message can be called God's power of salvation. Evidently the disclosure and acceptance of God's righteousness has power to deal effectively with the distorted human situation wherever it is accepted. Therein lies the gospel's promise. So we shall come back to this point.

Third, this rectifying work of God has not arrived on the scene belatedly, as an afterthought, but according to Rom 3:21 it has been and continues to be pointed to by scripture, precisely the scripture of the synagogue to which the Jews appeal in rejecting the gospel. Clearly there is a fundamental disparity between the way the synagogue reads the scripture and the way Paul reads it. Now if scripture bears witness to this rectification promised to those who believe, then this faith-righteousness is the heart of scripture. Miranda's book takes this with utmost seriousness. This is not the only valid Christian way of reading the Old Testament, but it is far more profound, exciting, and significant than reducing it to the background of the New Testament.

Fourth, Paul's audacious claim about scripture is grounded in the meaning of Jesus' execution and resurrection. Near the end of the highly compressed paragraph in Romans 3, Paul says, among other things, that this event occurred for the demonstration of God's righteousness—that is, so that God might disclose his rectitude and at the same time rectify whoever believes in the Christ event. In other words, the moral integrity of God manifests itself in rectifying the human situation. God is shown to be truly God when humanity is truly humanity. The righteousness of God creates righteousness on earth wherever the gospel is believed. This is the basis for Robert Jenson's observation that the gospel not only has a history—a history of interpretation and reformulation—but that it also creates history.[2] Where nothing is changed, the gospel has lost its potency—that is, it no longer manifests God's righteousness in such a way that the human situation begins to be rectified.

Finally, it becomes clear why getting in on this rectifying process depends on faith—not just faith or trust in general but the act of trusting the God who raised Jesus from the dead. At this point, we need to remember that our problem with resurrection of Jesus centers in the question whether such a thing as resurrection is necessary or possible. But the earliest Christians and Paul the Pharisee believed in resurrection long before they believed in Jesus. For them, it was not a question of whether such a thing is possible but whether it has happened, and whether it happened to Jesus. Moreover those Jews who believed in resurrection understood it to be one of the events at the hinge of history, when This Age would give way to the Age to Come, when creation would be restored, and God's will done on earth as it is in heaven. That is, the expected resurrection would inaugurate the new creation when everything would be right. To believe that Jesus had been resurrected, therefore, implied that the curtain was going up on the New Age. To believe that Jesus was resurrected implied that he was the criterion of the New Age. To believe this was to begin to get out of step with the present and into step with the dawning future.

II

With these basic considerations in mind, we are ready to appropriate important elements of our passage in Romans 10. First of all, the Jews' quest for righteousness, for rightness, is acknowledged to be fundamental. But seeking is not yet finding. Indeed Paul says that although Jews have a zeal for God they did not find God's righteousness and so undertook to establish their own. It is the zealous who failed. They did not discover that their quest for God's righteousness was a dead end, and so tried an alternative instead. Rather, the tragedy is that precisely in the zealous quest for God's righteousness they in fact unwittingly are establishing their own instead but think that it is God's.

This text has no word for us as long as we gentiles regard ourselves as superior to the Jews, or exempt from the process Paul is probing. The

---

2. Robert W. Jenson, *Story and Promise: A Brief Theology of the Gospel about Jesus* (Philadelphia: Fortress, 1973), 10.

fact is that the church cannot claim to be the people of God with one side of its mouth and at the same time declare itself exempt from the dangers of being God's people. Doubtless there are many ways in which also the church misses the righteousness of God precisely in its zeal, but our theme calls us to relate this phenomenon to the salvation offered in our evangelism. Precisely how that shakes out will become apparent as we proceed with the text.

In the next place, Paul declares that for those who believe the gospel, Christ is the end of the law as a way of righteousness. There is no concensus among exegetes on the question of whether the Greek term *telos* means end in the sense of termination, or whether it means end in the sense of goal. In some ways the debate is unreal, because if Christ is the goal of the law for those who believe, then he is at the same time its termination as the way of righteousness. Paul does not say simply, "Christ is the end of the law."

In the third place, from this standpoint Paul goes on to interpret Deuteronomy. Here a fundamental contrast is assumed, but only one side is actually formulated—namely, Moses writes concerning the righteousness which is grounded in the law, "The person who has done this righteousness shall live by it." At first this looks like a tautology, like saying that the person who has become an accomplished musician lives by music. In fact, however, it signals a self-contained world, a world in which righteousness is grounded in law, sought in law, and controlled by law. It will repay us to reflect briefly, all too briefly, on this point. Although some manuscripts insert the article it is likely that Paul wrote simply of law, not particularly of "the law," that is the law of Moses. Functionally, the law of Moses shares important features with law *qua* law, because fundamental to law is the nexus of obligation and doing. Obey your mother, Do what the teacher says, What do the regulations require? Go by the book, Obey the law. In other words, Paul cites Moses to say that whoever has achieved the obligation specified by law will in fact live by that kind of righteousness.

But what if the righteousness of law fails to produce the rectification by God? That question is at the heart of Paul's theology. But how can one say that following the law toward righteousness does not in fact lead to the goal? Paul deals with this question repeatedly, but without repeating himself. This means that the answer is complex and not simple. Two main reasons are important. One, the failure of law is disclosed objectively in the cross, because the law regards a crucified person as condemned. But if God resurrected a crucified Jesus and so delcared him to be the Lord and Christ, then the law is exposed as having denied what God affirms. Whoever believes in the resurrection of Jesus and lives by that can no longer trusts in law, for such a person the law as a way to God's righteousness has ended. Second, the subjective failure of the law is discussed in Romans 7, where Paul argues that the problem is not inherent in the law, at least not the law of Moses, for it is "just, holy and good." The reason this law cannot lead to righteousness and life is because another factor must be reckoned with, what Paul calls the law of sin and death. The problem is that we do not hear the law as neutrals, at zero point, free to do or not to do. When we hear the law we are already underway, already shaped by participation in sin and sin's power over us. Sinners cannot achieve what the law of Moses, or any other law for that matter, ultimately seeks—the total and pervasive rightness of all and things, and of persons' relations to one another/to God. The reality and power of sin thwarts the intent of the law and no amount of zeal for doing can overcome this.

The failure of the law to produce pervasive righteousness should be apparent to every person today. What actually happens is not the same as the intent and sometimes its opposite. We need to mention only such things as food stamps, public housing, social security and the like. Even if the legislation and the administrative procedures were perfect, much of what human greed would not distort, human sloth would frustrate. The righteousness of law must always settle for less than God's righteousness, and so ends up establishing its own proximate ends in place of total righteousness, and does so in the name of realism. In the name of realism, all talk of perfect righteousness is frequently dismissed as utopian. In this light, two critical observations are called for. One is against the tendency, exemplified by Miranda, to equate the law with codified civilization, a crystalized form of sin.[3] But Paul does not equate the law and sin, and even Miranda concedes this.[4] Nonetheless, he argues that for Paul law and faith are two epochs of history, and that "Paul wants a world without law"—i.e., a world without a state, as in Marxian thought. Actually, Paul wants a world without sin, in which the intent of the law—righteousness—will be realized and so make the law and the state unnecessary. In this Marx and Paul would agree but for Paul this is not an epoch of history, but a state of affairs which will replace what we call history. The

---

3. José Porfirio Miranda, *Marx and the Bible: A Critique of the Philosophy of Oppression*, trans. John Eagleson (1974; reprinted, Eugene, OR: Wipf & Stock, 2004), 182ff.

4. Ibid., 187.

other critical observation is aimed in the opposite direction—namely at those who use the failure of the law as an argument against law altogether. Wherever the slogan "You can't legislate morality" is the basis on which we refuse to legislate at all with regard to unrighteousness, there we end up sanctifying sin, indeed, worshipping it as the unchallengeable and unrestrainable lord of the earth.

We come back to the text now. Fourth, in contrast to the righteousness of the law, which is characterized by achievement, Paul turns to the righteousness which is grounded in faith. What strikes us at once is that he continues to quote the Pentateuch, yet does not attribute the words to Moses but to this alternative righteousness—as if it were a person. We shall bypass the fascinating exegetical possibilities which this poses, and deal with what this faith-rectitude says. It uses the language of Deuteronomy. But Paul reinterprets it dramatically. "Do not say in your heart, Who will ascend into heaven? Or who will decend into the abyss?"—that is the underworld where the dead are housed. In Deuteronomy, these lines have to do with the law—you need not go looking for God's will anymore. But Paul insists that they refer to Christ. The purpose of going to heaven is to bring Christ to earth; the purpose of going to the underworld is to bring him up to the earth. Why should one not do these things? Because the preached word, he continues, is present, the word which creates faith. It is in your mouth when you confess that Jesus is Lord and in your heart when you believe that God has already resurrected Jesus from the dead. That is, the righteousness of God is now on earth, and it is manifesting its presence and rectifying power wherever the preached word evokes confession of faith. That is why the gospel is the power of God's salvation. That is why the righteousness of God is revealed in it. The gospel can make good the promise of salvation because it is the bearer of God's rectification. The hallmark of the gospel is its power to subvert all unrighteousness and to generate in its place the aperatif of the final rightness of all things. Now we can see again why Jensen could say that the gospel makes history.

Is it an exaggeration to say that so much evangelism has lost its power because this dimension of the gospel is no longer understood? If I may paraphrase a few lines which come later in our passage, How shall persons be changed if the transforming word does not reach them? And how can it reach them if its bearers no longer understand it? And how can they understand it unless they discover afresh what its lineaments are, unless they exegete and theologize? As it has *not* been written, but may nonetheless be true of those pastors who take their work seriously, "How beautiful is the seat of those who sit at their desks from time to time."

Paul's use of the Old Testament here is more suggestive than commonly recognized. Three ideas merit some reflection: going up to heaven to bring Christ down, going down to the abyss to bring Christ up, and his being here already. It is often observed that the contrast of going up to heaven and going down to the abyss became a traditional Jewish way of speaking about what is impossible; even so, we should not overlook the fact that Paul does not use the tradition simply to say, Don't undertake the impossible.

The structure of the passage shows that the issue turns on whether Christ is absent or present on earth among humankind. This means that going up and going down are both to be set against the presentness borne by the kerygma and actualized in confessional faith. Nonetheless, going up and going down represent opposite alternatives to this presentness, and so we shall note each of them briefly.

What does it mean to try to go up to heaven to bring Christ down? If we remember that Christ and the righteousness of God go together, then it is evident that this attempt to bring Christ down is nothing less than an attempt to actualize utopia. It is the Promethean attempt to make the ideal, the ultimate rightness of things, actual. It is the attempt to transform the ideal into the real. What stands between us and the righteousness of God? It is the disparity between the ideal and the real. What does it take to overcome this? Effort. Paul's word is directed against precisely those modes of thought which say salvation would be real if we tried harder, planned better, spent more. He is equally opposed to the notion that such efforts could make Jesus Lord. Against this, Paul asserts that wherever Christ is confessed on earth as being Lord already, there the righteousness of God breaks forth. That is the Gospel's promise of salvation.

What does it mean to try to go down to the abyss to try to bring Christ up to us? Again, since Christ and the righteousness of God go together, it is clear that we are dealing with the attempt to pull the righteousness of God out of death, that is, to retrieve the righteousness of God from the ultimate fate of history. Christ was here once, but he went the way of all flesh. Salvation was real when he was alive. Ah, those were the good old days, when persons walked and talked to him, cast out demons, responded to parables. Much of Protestantism has wanted to bring back from the dead not only Christ but the early church as well. Salvation would be real if we could only resurrect the past. Against this, Paul asserts that wherever people believe that God has already resurrected Christ there salvation begins to occur. We do not need to make the historical Jesus relevant. Whenever one believes in the resurrection he is already relevant, because the resurrection is not some kind of miracle on Jesus' corpse but his vindication and manifestation as the one to whom we are accountable.

This is what it means to believe that God raised him from the dead and to confess that Jesus is Lord. Paul goes on to say that whoever believes in him will not be put to shame. The believer too will be vindicated. Ultimately this vindication occurs beyond death. But there is also a penultimate vindication, a preliminary, transient confirmation of faith within history. This occurs when the word of Christ's nearness to us passes from person to person and engenders faith in confession. This is what Miranda means, I think, when he speaks of the efficacy of faith and of the gratuitousness of faith, the grace-character of faith.[5] It is not the self-generated faith that makes us the outpost of the righteousness of God, but faith evoked by the shared word. This passing of the good news is what he describes as "horizontal causation." That is, "it is evangelization, begun by Jesus and continued by the church, which is God's instrument for causing faith and therefore justice in man." Wherever this flame spreads we are set free from acquiescing in the world as we know it. Wherever Jesus is confessed as Lord other lords are dethroned, and we can say No to the preeent in the name of God's Yes, that is, to his righteousness, his pledge to rectify truly a screwed up creation. It is true, of course, that Paul was convinced that this definitive rectification was imminent, and that nineteen centuries later we can no more resurrect his conviction by an act of will than we can resurrect Christ himself. Paul was wrong in when he expected this to happen, but he was not wrong in what he expected or whom he expected to bring it about. Still this is not the end of the matter. We are becoming more aware of how the picture of reality that we carry with us actually shapes the world we see, and how we live in it. The same is true of the story we tell. The Christian story includes a vision of God the rectifier. The plot of that vision embraces us when its story becomes our story and as the story is shared it becomes the story of others. Just as the visionary story of human history which Karl Marx told

---

5. Ibid., 174.

restructures reality and so creates history, so the Christian story restructures our worlds and sets in motion the rectification of the world.

Each year in Atlanta there occurs the annual celebration of Martin Luther King, the man with the dream. We know the eloquence with which he told the dream, and we know it energized him and what it cost him. We also know the result of sharing the dream. But where did he get the dream? In large part from his father, and where did he get it and those before him? It was the subversive story of the gospel which had been handed on and which continues to be told. Every act of redemption, every occurrence of rectitude, is part of the story though it be known only to God. To keep the story going is to facilitate the righteousness of God which occurs as gracious surprise again and again wherever people begin to believe that it is true and entrust themselves and the future to God's future. That is the gospel's promise of salvation.

PART 4

A Word for Bearers of the Word

Although these four presentations were made in academic settings, they neither report the latest trends in biblical scholarship nor explain why such things matter to the general public. Instead, these discourses, being addressed to the deeper needs of the church's leaders, are relentlessly theological. They show that theological exegesis is more than explaining biblical words and concepts—essential as that is—for it entails thinking theologically about the text's subjectt matter as expressed in its assertions.

The first is a sermon preached at Candler School of Theology at Emory University in Atlanta; the occasion was the convocation marking the beginning of the academic year 1976–77. The second, too, is a sermon for such an occasion, but this time in 1979, my first year as Dean at Yale Divinity School. It was published that fall in the school's journal, *Reflection*. The third piece, bearing a new title, was a lecture, also given at Candler, at the School's annual Ministers' Week, whose theme in 1982 was "The Gospel and the Minister." The fourth piece is a sermon given at Yale Divinity School's fall convocation in 1983, and was published in *Reflection* in 1984. Of the four, the third is the most demanding—and perhaps the most rewarding as well.

10

Our Identity's Dimensions

If anything has characterized theological education since the 60s it is perpetual self-examination and ceaseless experimentation. Nothing seemed to work right any more. The discipline of theology seemed simply to reflect the chaos of the culture. Sometimes the relationships between the faculty and their own teachers was as strained as that between the faculty and their students. No clear patterns of accountability seemed to survive the upheaval through which we have passed. The campuses are more quiet now, but the restless quest for an appropriate style and an adequate substance of theological education goes on without let-up. I suspect that more things are being tried simultaneously than ever before. Perhaps there was a time when seminaries could be sneered at as ivory towers amid ivied walls, but if so, they have long since been transformed into R and D centers with a pressure-cooker atmosphere. We have multiplied courses, learning situations, and styles of teaching. We have invented one degree program after another and have expanded the range of what is expected of all of us. At the same time, the students are expected to integrate what the faculty proliferates.

In this context we hear some lines from a writer who can be regarded as the first theologian to hammer out his theology in the churches long before there was an Institute of Church Ministries, the first theologian to be a pastoral counselor long before C.P.E. had been thought of (he probably would have flunked out anyway), the first Christian theologian who had to defend his identity long before an "identity crisis" was a fashionable thing to have. The theologian I have in mind is that irascible tentmaker from Tarsus, Paul. Listen to the words which are the text for our reflection:

> For the wisdom of this world is foolishness with God. For it is written,
> "He catches the wise in their craftiness,"
> and again,
> "The Lord knows the thoughts of the wise,
> that they are futile."
> So let no one boast about human leaders. For all things are yours, whether Paul or Apollos or Cephas or the world of life or death or the present or the future—all belong to you, and you belong to Christ, and Christ belongs to God.

If we are somewhat confused and perhaps a bit overwhelmed by everything going on around us and within us, this passage can clear our heads. It deals with three questions that accompany all our work together, and which cannot be evaded. Who is God? Who are the teachers who transmit the tradition? And, what is the structure of our accountability? Paul's answers are liberating.

I

All human knowledge is dogged by finitude, and human knowledge of God is no exception. No category, no vocabulary, no point of view, can achieve more than a finite expression of the elusive whole. But according to our text, the problem is deeper than the limitations of our theology. According to Paul, the decisive thing about theology is that its subject matter—God—not only transcends the categories and modalities of human thought but that he deliberately disavows them, mocks and explodes them. It is not so hard to live with the finitude of our knowing, but it is downright distressing to be told that the subject matter itself unmasks as folly what we have called wisdom. Now our defensive instincts urge us to conclude either that we have not heard the text aright, or that if we did, Paul is wrong. So let's look at the text first.

The text adapts the language of Job to speak of God as the one who catches, or traps, the wise in their craftiness. No concordance would help us find this understanding of God in the Bible because the word "God" is not used. Next, Paul appeals to Psalm 94, "The Lord knows the thoughts of the wise, that they are vain." Paul uses these Old Testament lines in order to show that what he is saying is not his own invention, not simply the expression of his own disillusionment with wisdom or his own alienation from it. His point was stated at the outset, "The wisdom of this world is foolishness with God." The wisdom of the world is not continuous with the wisdom of God, so that we could move easily from one to the other. Rather there is a fundamental contrast. The text declares the irreducible otherness of God.

In the presence of such a declaration we are tempted to say, "Yes, of course. That is the world's wisdom, but we have God's wisdom. Our theology is safe from this attack." We can even point to the previous chapter of our epistle in which Paul wrote, "We impart a secret and hidden wisdom of God," one which "God revealed to us through the Spirit." So we are on the side of the angels after all.

However, this misses the point. The wisdom of God revealed by the Spirit is the gospel of the cross and resurrection, not Christian theology. Christian theology is about that gospel, but Christian theology very much participates in the wisdom of this age for it is not the language of angels but of humans. Our language, our categories, our perceptions and perspectives all participate in the wisdom of this world. Christian theology is not answers revealed by God. Therefore the cross judges and exposes again and again not only the finitude but the folly of all our theologizing. When Christian theology is faithful to its subject matter, the God who is disclosed by the cross, it attempts to do justice to this otherness of God which God has planted in our midst by that gibbet at Jerusalem.

That may be what Paul means, we say, but surely he is wrong. To be sure, this is not the only thing Paul says about God, and what he says here is elicited by the drift of things in Corinth. Nonetheless, Paul was right. God is the one who does catch the wise precisely in their craftiness.

Does not the history of theology show that there is a boomerang effect, that things have a way of turning into their opposites? Perhaps some examples will help us see this more clearly. The Protestant Reformation got priests and nuns out of the cloistered orders into the world and we prided ourselves in the fact that this represented the sanctification of ordinary life and its pursuits. But now it appears that what began as a sanctification of the profane turned out to be a pervasive secularization of the holy which ended up by exiling the holy to the private dispositions of the self. Then in turn, the so-called secular man whose mentality was to be the norm of all things turned out to be the most gullible of all, buying as treasures what sophisticated minds have junked long ago. In the early nineteenth century, Hegel was hailed by some as the savior of Christian theology, for he regarded universal history as the saga of spirit actualizing itself. But then it turned out that precisely this drive toward a monistic explanation of all diversity was taken up by Marx and Engels in order to banish religion altogether and to argue that the driving force of history was not Spirit but matter, the means of production. In the twentieth century, Barth and Bultmann spoke about God on the basis of the self-authenticating word, but then it turned out this emphasis made the death of God theology inevitable once the word was heard no longer.

If that's the case, why not throw in the towel? Why not quit while we're ahead? What is more debilitating than learning in advance that nothing will succeed permanently? Actually, this word from Job and Paul is an emancipation proclamation for theologians. It liberates us from two things at least. First, it frees us from the idolatry that seeps in when we think our theology has been revealed. Every pastoral counselor knows what sort of hang-ups occur when commitment to God is simply equated with attachment to a theology, a doctrine, a precious phrase. Liberation occurs when we learn to distinguish trusting in God from trusting a statement about God, because enslavement occurs when the one is collapsed into the other. In short, we are truly justified by faith, not at all by our belief in justification by faith.

Second, this disconcerting word frees us from a compulsive need to get it right, from the anxiety that if our theology should be off-base or not eternally true, we have blown it. I once experienced this sort of liberation I am talking about. I was on the threshold of my teaching career, and although I had a freshly minted PhD I was anxious about finding the right way to begin the sophomore course in Bible, which began of course with Old Testament. But the chairman of the department gave me freedom when he said, "All ways are wrong. Now let's try to find the one that works best for you." From then on, I was truly free to try.

So in all our theologizing, we strive to achieve the best not because we are anxious about our security but because the subject matter elicits from us nothing less than our best. But we don't have to make it perfect. After all, the God who forgives the sinner will also forgive the theologian.

II

The second question addressed by our text is, Who then are the teachers of our theological tradition? It is not a question of learning their names, but their roles. It was this question which provoked Paul in to writing this part of the epistle in the first place, for the Corinthians were sorting themselves out by saying, "I am of Paul, I am of Apollos, I am of Cephas." Our text is only part of Paul's response. Even so, there is more than enough to occupy us.

On occasions like this, an opening convocation, it is customary to emphasize that we are all students, united in a common quest for knowledge, truth, and wisdom. Fine. But our text calls upon us to reflect upon the relation between student and teacher in light of what has already been said about the relation to the subject matter. And this involves all of us because those who are enrolled as students have teachers, and we teachers ourselves have our teachers. What is being discussed here is the relation between student and teacher across the board.

Paul was too realistic to pretend that teachers are interchangeable parts. Teachers usually differentiate themselves from one another even if the students do not. After all, individuality is part of our stock in trade. The problem is not that teachers are different, nor that students have preferences.

The problem lies deeper, on that level where the relation between teacher and student becomes tyrannous. This can develop from either end. Sometimes teachers cultivate a clientele, a sect of intensely loyal students who are encouraged to seal themselves off from contaminating influence of other teachers. This mentality takes an institutionalized turn when departments become overly possessive of their students, discourage them from taking courses elsewhere in order to protect their fiefdoms. Sometimes it is the students who become so attached to a teacher that they regard themselves as their disciples. To be sure, where there are deep differences, choices must be made. When I was a graduate student in Göttingen, there were two seminars in New Testament each term and they met at the same time so that one had to choose Käsemann or Jeremias. No student could serve two masters there. But what I am really getting at however is that lifelong dependence on the teacher which makes one either a parrot who repeats, or a scholastic who refines the answers without asking questions.

The fascinating thing about our text is the fact that although Paul is one of those who has a powerbase in Corinth so to speak, he seems hellbent on dismantling it. Not a word of criticism of Cephas nor hint of a sneer against the competence of Apollos. Nothing to make him look good at their expense, or to enhance his clique at the expense of theirs.

Instead, he transforms the whole situation by reversing the language. The people in Corinth say, "I belong to Paul" or "I belong to Apollos," but Paul says Paul, Apollos, and Cephas *belong to you*. Thereby he emancipated everyone, teachers and students alike, from tyrannous relationship. This text is a summons for maturity which none of us has reached. What I hear in this text is Paul's bugle calling us to freedom to appropriate the whole rich legacy of the Christian tradition precisely in its diversity. This is why the key phrase is, "All things are yours." Why encapsulate yourself with a part when it all belongs to you? You do not belong to the part. The part belongs to you. Why not claim it? Why insist on a sectarian appropriation of the Christian tradition? If no theology can be regarded as the God-given revelation but only as the human attempt to speak clearly and consistently about it, why should anyone insist on being defined by a transient and finite part? It all belongs to all of us.

Shall I be more specific? Twenty years ago, an American at Marburg and I joined a tour group to Italy. When we visited the Vatican my friend enjoyed confusing the guide by saying that he was a Catholic Methodist. The guide of course insisted that there was no such thing; but Jerry was claiming the whole Christian legacy as his birthright. There is nothing more fundamental to the elan, the spirit, the ethos of a theological school than this vocation of replacing every Christian parochialism with a sense of the catholic whole.

Shall I be specific again? I take it that one reason we have found it necessary to develop the Institute of Church Ministries, to go into local congregations to teach and to learn, is that we have forgotten how to appropriate and transmit the legacy that has come down to us in books. What an indictment! Perhaps we treated Calvin as if he were all distilled into the *Institutes*; Schleiermacher as if he were embodied in his systematic theology, *The Christian Faith*; Barth as if were imprisoned in the *Church Dogmatics*. Have we forgotten where these persons wrought their theologies? Have we so intellectualized and abstracted the tradition from the living tissue of people that we think the problems of congregations in metropolitan Atlanta are really more significant, more productive for learning and teaching, than those faced by the churches for which Augustine, Calvin, Barth, or Bonhoeffer wrote? If we do, we show that we have killed the tradition by the way we have packaged it. I hope that the Institute experiences will evoke from us a fresh discovery of the legacy in our library. If we do not claim our legacy, we are like a family who inherited a mansion but lives in one room and insists that after all, you don't need the rest anyway. If, on the other hand, we claim our legacy, if we believe that all these things belong to us, then Paul and Augustine, Francis and Anselm, Luther and Bunyon and Wesley will belong to us the way we belong to one another. They will not be simply the church fathers but the church brothers, and we may discover some sisters too. Then the books will be the paths to our peers.

Claiming a legacy as rich and diverse as ours need not end in an indiscriminate eccleticism in which we say Yes to everything and No to nothing. It need not produce a spineless existence in which one's thoughts are determined by the book read last. Rather, it should, and can, yield a discerning freedom to claim whatever enriches and nurtures us in the Christian faith. It should, and can, induce us to make some judgments, to find our identity vis-à-vis a wider circle of alternatives. The arrival of 4-1/2 miles of books announces the presence of an immense legacy.[1] "All things are yours." They belong to us, however, only if we claim them.

III

The third question that is answered here is, What is the structure of accountability? Our text continues, "All things belong to you, but you belong to Christ and Christ belongs to God." Here is a structure of belonging which brings with it a pattern of accountability. The one to whom nothing is foreign or off limits, the one to whom all things belong, in turn belongs to another. Christians are sovereign but not autonomous, we belong to a Lord to whom we are accountable.

We are not accustomed to think of belonging and accountability together. Even less do we expect to find our quest for both fulfilled in the same place. We tend to seek belonging in order to satisfy our need for security and community. At the same time we avoid accountability in the name of doing our own thing, fulfilling ourselves at all costs, as if every self ought to be fulfilled because it lives in Eden and not east of it, as if we were Adam and Eve before the fall. We fail to see that on this basis there can only be a choice between belonging and self-actualization. In other words, the flight from accountability makes it impossible for us to belong, and the quest for belonging cannot be fulfilled so long as we have no one to whom we are accountable. When husband and wife belong

---

1. Candler's Pitts Library had recently received Hartford Theological Seminary's library, purchased by Emory University.

to one another, each is accountable to the other. When children know they belong in a family and do not merely sleep in the house, they know they are accountable to their parents and their parents are accountable to them. In the home, as soon as one declares that there is no more accountability to the other, then belonging is destroyed as well. To belong is to be accountable.

To belong to Christ is to be in a specific sphere of power and meaning in which the world is being restored as creation. That is why the person who belongs to Christ can lay claim to all things, because through Christ God is reclaiming the world. But if the place of belonging marks also the place of accountability, then we are accountable to God's Christ. And for what are we accountable? For precisely what we do with all things that are ours. Here too the word of Jesus applies, "To whom much is given, of him or her shall much be required." No aspect of our existence lies outside the range of accountability because the total self of all of us belongs to Christ.

What Paul is alluding to is what we might call Christomorphic life, a life shaped by Christ. In this life, theology is a series of attempts to give a coherent account of this process, and the teachers of theology are but resources or models for how it has been undertaken. We are accountable in the last instance only to the one to whom we belong and we do not belong to anyone but the Christ and even he is not autonomous for he belongs to God. Here we get it all together at last.

IV

None of us knows what this year will bring, or for that matter, take away. But what does it matter? If we belong to Christ and if he belongs to God, then we can be free enough of anxiety about ourselves and our future to go to work. What are we waiting for?

11

A Word for Us Theologians
(Romans 12:1–2)

Occasions like this invite us to ponder afresh what is rudimentary, what is constitutive, what is so valid that it must be appropriated again and again. What we need most right now is not a policy statement from a new dean but a word from an apostle, a word that reminds us of who we are, what we are about, and what that amounts to. Listen with me, then, for the word of God as it may come to us through the opening sentence of the twelfth chapter of the Letter to the Romans:

> I appeal to you therefore, brethren—and sisters—by the mercies of God, to present your bodies as a living sacrifice, holy and acceptable to God, which is your spiritual worship. Do not be conformed to this world but be transformed by the renewal of your mind, that you may prove what is the will of God, what is good and acceptable and perfect.

This compacted sentence hands us the key to our identity, clarifies our task, and lifts our eyes to the horizons.

I

The horizon comes into view when we ask, what is the goal, the *telos* of our knowing? What is the theological enterprise all about? What does it amount to? Given the richness of our diversity, we shall not answer this question in a monolithic way.

Remarkably, there is a constant, a thread which weaves its way through the multicolored tapestry of our answer, namely, that theology is our central task. Theological education that is not grounded in and shaped by theological understanding and conviction becomes, a mere hodgepodge of courses and learning-experiences, a chattering about God and humanity without center, coherence, or high purpose beyond ourselves. Each of us, whatever his or her craft or specialty, is a theologian, interpreting and focusing the gospel. The explication of the gospel for the sake of the gospel in the church and the world is a vocation from which none of us is exempt. In whatever form or with whatever accent, theology is our business.

But what is the horizon of this effort? What does it amount to? If we are open to our text, we hear a trenchant answer, for the Apostle ends with a statement of purpose which is remarkably germane—"that you may prove what is the will of God."

At first we shrink back. It's not an answer we are prepared to hear. The will of God may not be part of our working vocabulary. We know how often the will of God has been the slogan for fanaticism. We know that there is too much cheap talk about God's will when a child gets leukemia. Is the horizon of our theological effort really the will of God?

As a matter of fact, it is precisely the repeated abuse of the phrase that puts it on our agenda and keeps it there. In other words, the agenda of our theologizing is set not simply by the latest book written by a theologian, important as that may be; our agenda is set also by the ways in which God is talked about, appealed to, cursed and ignored by ordinary folk. What I am pointing to is the pastoral and prophetic function of theology within the Christian community and beyond it. When measured by one set of criteria, our culture and our churches appear to be thoroughly secularized. When gauged by other criteria, the scene appears to be marked by pervasive religiosity and superstition, adamant and shrill demands that this or that must be done—all of which are but disguised appeals to the will of God, the ultimate obligation, the necessary course of things to be followed. One has only to check how commonly books, sermons, speeches use the word "must." To be responsible theologians is to discern the many forms which the appeal to God's will takes today, and to assess them critically in light of the gospel.

Once we begin to think along these lines, it comes clear that recent theology itself has been dominated by the will of God, whether or not the phrase was used. In our time, theology has been turned into a rationale for a program to be achieved, an ideational sub-structure to legitimate an emphasis. So we have been treated to a theology of joy, a theology of play, a theology of sex, a theology of ecology. But it is one thing to discern the import of theology for the actualities in which we find ourselves; it is another to cut, plane and fit the understanding of God into the role of the ultimate sanction for programs, even ones we espouse. In such theologizing the reality we call God is deprived of its freedom and integrity, turned into a transcendant yes to what we know and demand, and into a transcendant no to whatever we oppose. Such a God can no longer be against us, and would never die for those who oppose us. So the will of God is on our agenda for the sake of the integrity of theology itself. To be responsible theologians is to be critical of theology, lest the mystery of God become domesticated.

There is yet a third reason why the will of God is the horizon of our theological work, and this has to do not so much with what is advocated in God's name as it does with what is assumed. No one has opened our eyes more to this tacit appeal to God's will than have the women, the minorities and the wretched poor. It is easy enough for white middle-class male theologians to point out the ideological excesses which sometimes mark this protest theology, but who of us has not learned embarrassing things about ourselves and what we assumed was God's will?

I have been reflecting on various aspects of this theme of God's will because it alerts us to the disturbing insight that all our talk of God is marked by "interest," a sense of having a stake in our talk of God. The burgeoning field of the sociology of knowledge may help us get that into focus. In any case, what I have been leading up to is this—that the will of God is the horizon of our theological work because knowledge of God has an irreducible moral dimension. There is no disinterested talk of God, for by definition God is the One in whom all our trusts are grounded, our values anchored, and at the same time, the One who stands out against us as the Holy One, that is, the One in whom integrity and power coincide. On this side of Auschwitz, Dresden, Wounded Knee, the Gulag Archipelago, and Vietnam, surrounded by humanity exploited and debased, to talk about God and to pray to God, without reckoning with the will of God is to engage in blasphemy.

But given the loose talk, the special interest pleading and the fanaticism, does not the Apostle make matters worse by implying that the goal of our theological work is "proving" the will of God? Not really, for Paul's word does not mean proving in the sense of a court of law, but proving out as in the assayist's jar. It has to do with the testing out by trial. It embraces a note of uncertainty. What Paul's word legitimates is not the hybris of the knower but modesty and humility. He does not speak of knowing God's will at all, but of probing for it in the light of a gospel of God's mercy. Just before he dictated our text, he had said of God's ways, "How unsearchable are his judgements and how inscrutable his ways." Only when that is seen clearly can we grasp rightly the paradoxical summons to discern the will of God whose ways are finally hidden—even from (or should I say especially from?) us theologians.

Theology, you see, is the perpetual probing of mystery and reflection on mystery. It is not our task to explain the mystery but to explain why it remains mystery, precisely in revelation. It is in the presence of this fact that we at Yale Divinity School are poised on the edge of opportunity, for the presence of the arts invites us to acknowledge and celebrate the mystery, to enter the funding myths through the imagination and the feelings, lest we reduce everything to concepts—carefully pruned of ambiguity. The language of the heart and the grammar of the imagination allow us to live in the presence of mystery and to celebrate its presence as persons. The possibility for this community to engage in serious and significant theology in both the analytical, conceptual mode and in the imaginative mode must not be missed.

Pursuing theology whose *telos*, whose horizon, is the will of God summons us all to the best, and nothing short of the best. Given the state of theology, the state of the church and the state of humanity, our best will be scarcely good enough.

II

If so much is required of us, how shall we proceed? Or, to put our second question more broadly, what shall be the ethos of our learning? The Apostle's word is quite direct. "Be not conformed to this world (that is, to this age) but be transformed by the renewal of the mind." The discerning of God's will is to be the outgrowth of non-conformity and transformation which flows from renewing the mind.

That sounds easy enough: be deviant and think differently. In the dusk of the 70s, there is enough of the 60s around to help us understand what is called for—a starting point and a way of thinking which is not derived from the given and the inherited. Remember the in-words "drop

A WORD FOR US THEOLOGIANS

out" and "counter-culture"? They signalled the attempt to break out of conformity with our culture. Concern for mind-renewal appears to have a longer lifespan, especially since our culture has become ever more narcissistic. Want ads offer a rich assortment of ways to renew, expand, transform and tap the mind. Those parents whose teenagers have had their minds transformed can hire deprogrammers. One movement after another wants to raise our consciousness. So deep has gone this demand for disengagement from the past that we have been urged to think disparagingly of the mind itself, to release and revel in feelings. An occupant of a distinguished chair in theology once ventured to do theology as a body, and published reflections on his penis floating in the bathtub. Running through this plethora of revolt is the recognition that what we think, where we think, how we think and with what metaphors and categories we think really do determine who we are, what we can see and what we shall do. Despite the bizarre and the banal which we have witnessed, our recent past should at least alert us to the truth of what the Apostle says—that transformation by the renewal of the mind is fundamental to discerning the will of God.

The import of this insight for our work together has many levels, but let me focus on one which pertains to the question I raised a moment ago—the ethos of our learning. Transformation by the renewal of the mind lies at the heart of theological education, for administration and faculty no less than for students. But this truth is difficult to translate into style and substance. Given the alleged knowledge explosion, given the proliferation of forms of ministry, and given the apparently infinite range of possibilities of combining inquiries, considerable wisdom is required to distinguish that which truly renews the mind from that which merely clutters it. But rarely is the mind renewed and the self transformed quantitatively—by simply adding courses. The pertinence of the Christian faith to the whole of life does not translate directly into courses on everything.

What renews the mind and transforms the self is sustained engagement with seminal ideas, reflective conversation with significant persons, past and present, coupled with the assimilation of powerful images and myths. Concretely, this implies that the mind of the Christian theologian is renewed and she herself is transformed by penetrating and pondering the funding rudiments of the Christian faith and the clearest insights of the tradition. The self is transformed and the mind renewed when Isaiah and Paul, Augustine and Wesley, Martin Luther and Martin Luther King become our predecessors and peers, sharing pilgrimage and ecstasy. But would it not be ironic if we learned to converse with our predecessors and peers in the past but failed to do so with our contemporaries—student with student, student with faculty, faculty with faculty?

The mind is renewed and the self transformed not simply by attending to what these persons have affirmed but especially by entering into what they asked and learning why and how their asking it became fruitful. When the legacy of questions is shared, the tradition is no longer a burden but an inheritance to be claimed. It is nothing short of tragic that the church, including so many of its leaders, gives the impression that it is camping out in a mansion it has inherited but does not know how to inhabit with freedom and gratitude. For our life and labor together, the transformation by the renewal of the mind requires of us the best scholarship of which we are capable. What the horizons of the will of God for humanity, the concrete needs and hurts of people, and the malaise of much of the church demand from us is not less scholarship but more, not easy answers but profound questions which bear their fruit in due season. The transformation and the renewal will occur most significantly when the scholarly penetration of a tradition occurs among those who are cornmited to discerning the will of God in the world today.

III

This brings me to the third question on our minds—what shapes our identity? What is it that forms us into effective and articulate leaders of the people of God? The opening line of our text supplies an answer -though it may not be one for which we are prepared: "Present your bodies - the actual selves we are—as a living sacrifice," and goes on to observe that this is our proper worship (which the RSV obscures by rendering it "spiritual worship"). The Apostle is not speaking of the immolation of the self, the repression of the body or the amputation of any of its drives. What he is urging is the ongoing process by which the self, the whole self, is made holy.

The self is not made holy by repression but by hallowing the whole, for things and persons are made holy by being brought into relation to the Holy One, by the right ordering of the self in relation to its Ground. Given the shape and misshape of our selves, this process entails repentance, a word not in Paul's vocabulary but which he surely knew. Repentance is not regret for failing to be religious sooner. Rather, repentance is the discipline of turning life Godward and holding it steadily into the wind. And this, our text implies, is our proper worship—the hallmark of true service to God. What, then, shapes our identity? It is the process of ever anew making ourselves available to God for service. It is the praxis of trusting God with the whole self, not just comprehending God with the mind nor just doing God's will with hands and feet. This may be as disconcerting as it is demanding, for it disallows any bifurcation of life into cerebral acuity and body ethic. It permits no convenient hiatus between mental power and moral character. It summons to integrity, to wholeness. It suggests that serious theology and significant ministry are alike grounded in the surrender of the self to God.

This relation to God is not achieved all at once, nor all alone. Therefore our text implies that worship together is at the heart of a theological community. It implies that the renewal of the mind will be but a mental masturbation if it is not linked with commitment to the gospel that alone perpetually transforms us for the seeking and doing of God's will. It implies that the core matrix of our theological endeavor is not culture but worship, in which we are sustained and renewed.

IV

So our text summons us all to a quality of life and a style of work which is grounded in self-entrustment to the God of the gospel, a quality of life and a style of work which seeks the renewal of the mind guided by predecessors and peers, to a quality of life and a style of work oriented to the discerning of God's will for a confused church and a bleeding humanity. As Paul put it elsewhere, our text summons us—all of us—to work out our salvation with fear and trembling—to risk allowing the gospel to come true in us.

Who is up to that? None of us. And all of us. None of us because it is more than we are able to achieve on our own, by simply setting our jaws and going at it. All of us because each in his or her own way is enabled, by the gracious empowering presence of God, to begin, and to be faithful to what each has been given in Christ.

This shaping and reshaping of life and labor will proceed gradually, perhaps painfully, if we allow this text and the gospel in which it is rooted, to inform us. What Paul wrote to the Philippians he could have written precisely to us as well: "I am sure that he who began a good work in you will bring it to completion at the day of Jesus Christ."

Those who live by this promise will become theologians—the interpreters of the divine mystery into the concrete—and the bearers of grace through their ministry. You can count on it.

12

Is There Good News for Ministers Too? (Romans 8)

The title of this address does not say very much about its content or scope. This is because announcing a title before the address is written is like naming the baby when it is conceived. Now that delivery time is at hand, it is useful to reflect on what the name—that is, the title—turns out to mean.

To begin with, the word "minister" is used in a wide sense because if one thing has become clear in our time it is the difficulty of working with a narrow, precisely-defined understanding of the word "minister." It is mostly Protestants who refer to their clergy as "the minister," a usage whose problems we have not overcome. If "ministering"—being of service—is incumbent on all Christians in virtue of their baptism, then there is something odd about speaking of certain persons as "the ministers," and it is not surprising that we have been speaking of "the ministry of the laity"—as if that validated them! Moreover, nowadays laypersons do everything the ordained clergy do except the sacramental acts, and even this turns out to be ambiguous when we recall that Roman Catholic laity can baptize and that Campbellite laity can preside at the Table. So when I speak of "the minister" I do not restrict the scope of these remarks to the ordained, nor to the pastors of churches, but include the church bureaucrat, the chaplain, the Director of Christian Education, the Minister of Music, the academic whose sense of vocation embraces a ministry; in short, I am thinking of all of us in solidarity with all Christians insofar as we are engaged in ministering.

PART 4: A WORD FOR BEARERS OF THE WORD

The theme of gospel and the minister has in view something that is both intimately personal and seriously theological, namely, how the Christian message impinges on the ministering person. In a way, the question with which we shall be concerned is this—Is there good news for the minister? If there is a crisis in what we call "the ministry," it has to do with precisely this question.

We are not the first ministers to reflect on this theme. Indeed, the oldest parts of the New Testament—the Letters of Paul—grapple with it repeatedly. So it is to Paul that I want to direct our attention. But I shall not concentrate on those letters or parts of letters in which Paul clarifies and defends his ministry. There are two reasons for this decision. One is because Paul's ministry had an unrepeatable quality to it—he regarded himself as the last of the apostles (because with him the resurrection appearances ended) and as the apostle to the gentiles at a decisive and unrepeatable point in time. The second reason for bypassing sections where Paul reflects on his apostolic ministry is that it allows us to bring to bear on ministry considerations which Paul regards as true of all Christians, irrespective of function or what we call rank and role. The theme of "Gospel and the Minister," after all, cannot be isolated from the gospel's promise and claim on every Christian. So we will probe Romans 8.

After orienting ourselves to the situation in which we find ourselves, I will select certain elements of Romans 8 to serve a double function—to deepen our perception of where we are and at the same time to deal with what is exposed. I am aware, as are you, that Romans is not all of Paul, and that Paul is not the whole New Testament. I am also persuaded that more than any of his contemporaries, Paul has a word for us.

I

The situation in which we find ourselves has been diagnosed and excoriated so many times, and from so many angles, that anyone who read and believed it all would certainly slide into deep depression. It is not my intent to poormouth ministers; it is, instead, to call attention to two aspects of our situation which, I suspect, play significant parts in generating the dilemmas of ministry to which the theme of this Ministers Week is addressed. What I will say is only a reminder of what we already know rather than a discovery of which you need to be informed; still it will orient our thinking to remember these two things .

A. The first concerns *The diminished sense of the holy*, which is but the correlate of the ascendency of secularity. Not even those churches that continue to say their ordained clergy receive "Holy Orders" have escaped the acid rain of secularity. The ministry, ordained or not, has become secularized—that is, lost its sense of the holy—to a degree that might surprise our forebears. Nothing attests more convincingly that our sense of the holy, the sacred and the transcendant, has been diminished than do our multiple efforts to retrieve it. The so-called "charismatic movement" is but a vivid and accessible mark of such efforts. The current popularity of books, weekend seminars, and seminary courses dealing in some way with "spirituality" is also a sign that we miss the sacred, the holy, the spiritual.

The same thing takes a quite different form–the pervasive utilitarianism which pervades the entire life of the church. I want to say a word more about this. What I have in mind is the propensity of the pragmatic mind which is preoccupied with sanctification to turn the gospel into useable power. I need not justify characterizing the American mind as pragmatic. Concern for what is practical, for what works best, is basic to our approach to reality, and all technological societies give a commercial value to this concern as well. American Protestantism, furthermore, has been preoccupied consistently with what is known in dogmatics as "sanctification," with the good effects of salvation. Many Americans will believe anything or try anything if it will bring about a better life. We regard the gospel as a resource for achieving goals, as an answer to a set of problems. Not surprisingly, we created the phrase "applied Christianity," parallel to "applied mathematics." Inevitably, ministering has come to mean "applying." Inevitably, the gospel becomes less and less the good news which the minister hears and shares, and more and more an ideology, a policy or a strategy which the minister advocates. The cliché is not as popular now as it was recently, but the substance remains, namely, the minister as a "change agent." So-called " liberation theology" seems to have consecrated this secularized understanding of the ministry, probably unintentionally, by adopting Marxist jargon about "praxis," thereby also warding off critics who do not share the same starting-point. In any case the current forms of utilitarianism in the church manifest themselves in many ways, not least of which is the desire to instruct the gospel about what it may and must say before we find it useful for our projects.

B. If we remember that holiness and wholeness go together, then it should not surprise us that the diminished sense of the holy brings with it a *loss of wholeness*, a fragmentation, a sense that the pieces do not cohere the way we surmise they should. With no transcendant center, which gives coherence to the parts, we know ourselves pulled apart and so we struggle for integration. Wherever our ministries may take place, we find ourselves to be factored into segments, all of which we want to affirm. Lacking a life-giving and hallowing center, we yield to the multiple demands of good things. I have often quipped that we are being killed by good things, good causes, good involvements, good activities. Inevitably what we value more and more is "getting it all together." The black-bound book by which we live is not so much the Bible as it is the little datebook, crammed full of engagements, often meetings to plan meetings. For years, the little magazine which Boston University School of Theology sent to its graduates contained a feature concerning the activities of the faculty—their lecturing, participation in commissions, preaching and writing. The title of the section was, I suspect, more a pious hope than a statement of reality, for this title combined what many of us experience mostly as contradiction—"Holiness and Hustle." But even so, it is not wholeness. The point is that the loss of wholeness brings about the frenetic life. We find ourselves to be so busy being relevent in the kitchen with Martha that we have little time to join Mary in the presence of the Lord.

What I am pointing toward is the sense of the holy which gives a sense of wholeness, the sacred which discloses the connectedness of things and so puts the particular into perspective. This was real to the prophet of the social gospel, Walter Rauschenbusch. Do you recall these lines?

> In the castle of my soul
> Is a little postern gate,
> Whereat, when I enter,
> I am in the presence of God.
> In a moment, in the turning of a thought,
> I am where God is.
> This is a fact.
>
> When I enter into God
> All life has a meaning,
> Without asking I know;
> My desires are even now fulfilled,
> My fever is gone.

> In the quiet presence of God.
> My troubles are but pebbles on the road,
> My joys are like the everlasting hills.
>
> So it is when my soul steps through the postern gate
> Into the presence of God.
> Big things become small and small things become great.
> The near becomes far and the future is near.
> The lowly and despised is shot through with glory . . .
> When I am in Him I am in the Kingdom of God
> And in the Fatherland of my soul.

I read these lines not to make us feel more guilty than we feel already, but to remind us that without what Rauschenbusch called "the quiet presence of God," the sense of the holy in our midst which sanctifies the whole, the much doing of good soon becomes empty and the doer dies. If this is true, then the way toward wholeness and the holy is neither a matter of eliminating activities, like going on a diet, nor a matter of adding one more thing—the zealous quest for a special holy thing, act or experience alongside everything else. As one writer put it recently, the holy "is not an object alongside other objects, but rather a field made up from all reality." God is holy not only because God is other, but also because being God means being intimately connected with the whole of reality.[1] As Rauschenbusch put it, "When I enter into God, all life has meaning"—note that he did not say that everything is explained. Rather, in God the One is grounded the life-giving wholeness which we can never formulate and explain but which we know is there, and know so deeply that we can affirm ambiguity and absurdity. This is why the language most appropriate to discourse about the holy is myth, for myth bends language to say the unsayable which must be said.

If this be true, then the vocation of the exegete, whether in the pulpit or at the lectern, is not to demythologize the language of myth into timeless abstractions which the mind can affirm, but rather to make it accessible, having first allowed oneself to enter it and to claim it and to be claimed by it. If this be true, then ministry cannot be reduced to an agenda of good projects without becoming a parody of true ministration to the human condition; then ministry becomes transformed into

---

1. Gerd Theissen, *A Critical Faith: A Case for Religion*, trans. John Bowden (Philadelphia: Fortress, 1979), 53, 33.

a sharing of a vision of the interconnectedness of all things which may open out onto the holy which we know but cannot define. If this be true, then the remainder of this address will not exhort you to "take time out to be holy," if I may paraphrase a gospel song, nor attempt to generate the experience of the holy; it will rather invite you to see with me what Paul saw and struggled to say. If we can make some progress toward that, then I believe we will have an affirmative answer to the question with which we began, "Is there good news for the minister?" Then too we may find a crust of bread to nourish us on the road.

II

In Romans 8 Paul brings to a moving climax the first part of his magisterial epistle. We may leave aside just now many of the problems with which it keeps New Testament critics employed and publishers in business. We shall, instead, concentrate on four passages where our own loss of the sense of connectedness might be healed.

A. The first passage consist of verses 2 through 4: "For the law of the Spirit of life in Christ Jesus has set me free from the law of sin and death. For God has done what the law, weakened by the flesh, could not do: sending his own Son in the likeness of sinfull flesh and for sin, he condemned sin in the flesh, in order that the just requirement of the law might be fulfilled in us, who walk not according to the flesh but according to the Spirit."

In a remarkable way, these two sentences, hold together what we customarily tear apart: The human condition, the christological event as God's response, law, and the new life under the aegis of the divine Spirit. This is not simply a list of theological themes, let alone doctrines, which ought to be related to one another. Rather, it is a tightly formulated vision of reality.

For our purposes, we will concentrate on the surprising way in which Paul holds together law and Spirit. In chapter 7 Paul appears to have said quite the opposite, namely, that "now we are discharged from the law, dead to what held us captive, so that we serve not under the old written code but in the new life of the Spirit"—at least that is how the RSV has it.

What is more popular, especially today, than this alternative between the law and the Spirit ? Who will not applaud this emancipation from law, structures and codes of obligations or requirements, and hail enthusiastically the new life of the Spirit? Who can measure the mischief done through anti-Semitism which in part rests on the assumption that the Jews live by a religion of laws but Christianity, thank God, is a spiritual religion? How often has Paul's emphasis on justification by faith rather than by works of the law been construed to mean that the gospel emancipates us from law categorically. "Love God and do as you like" has been a popular slogan. But now on the very next page Paul seems to take it all back, for here he writes of "the just requirement of the law" being fulfilled in us who walk ... according to the Spirit."

On closer examination, it turns out that Paul expresses himself more carefully, and thinks with more subtlety, than we expect. In Chapter 7, he writes of being freed from the law as letter, as written code of obligations which we strive to fulfill but cannot; in Chapter 8 he writes of "the just requirement of the law," as the RSV translates it—a difficult line which I would paraphrase as "what the law is all about." In other words, the emancipation of which Paul writes is not from obligation categorically but from a hopeless condition in which we pervert the law because we are captive to flesh and to the illusion that we can do what is required. This is why in our passage he writes that the law was "weakened by the flesh." The Spirit, then, is not inherently opposed to what the law is all about; rather, the Spirit is opposed to the flesh because both are fields of force in which one lives—somewhat like opposing magnetic fields. This is why Paul goes on to write, "Those who are in the flesh cannot please God," as well as to declare, "you are not in the flesh, you are in the Spirit." That is, you have been transferred from one domain to another. Once we see this, we see also how perverse is the translation of the New English Bible, which renders "flesh" as "our lower nature"—as if the struggle between Spirit and flesh were a struggle between our higher and lower natures, between God's Spirit and our spirit s on the one side, and our sheer physicality on the other.

When Paul joins the Spirit and "the just requirement of the law" he is not saying that those who have the Spirit can now achieve the obligations of the written code which was impossible before, because that would imply that the difference between pre-Christian and Christian existence is really a matter of receiving a special additive (the Spirit) which makes us more successful than before. Because we interpret Paul this way, we end up advocating a monstrous Christian life—one that is essentially Spirit-sanctioned legalism and moralism—as if justification by faith alone were a cheap way to play the same game. The point rather is those who entrust themselves to God on the basis of the gospel receive the empowerment of the Spirit, and accordingly do what the law is all about, not in order to get right with God but because the relation to God is already rectified. Paul does not spell out the content of "the just requirement of the law" but later in this Letter he declares that "love is the fulfilling of the law" (13:10), and that whoever loves the neighbor has fulfilled the law (13:8).

How shall we appropriate this ? How is this interconnectedness of obligation and Spirit a word of good news for ministers? Two implications suffice to point the way. *First*, the minister, no less than any person, is justified by faith, has one's relation to God rectified by sheer and simple trust in God. The minister is freed from the compulsion to prove that he or she is more loving, more caring, more effective than anyone else because after all he or she is the professional Christian. No more need to be the super-Christian perpetually, no more passion to increase our stature (as Jesus put it) because one is theologically educated (perhaps even with C.P.E.) and perhaps ordained. No more need to prove anything except to manifest the freedom to love truly, to weep with the weeping and to dance with those who rejoice (as Paul almost put it) because one's existence and relation to God are not at stake in our achievement. In short, what Paul shows us is the alternative to the secularization of the ministry, which manifests itself in our sliding back in to a mode of life distinguishable from any other so-called "helping profession" only by being connected to the church. Nothing, I am convinced, would renew ministers more than rediscovering the liberating power of justification by faith.

Here a word needs to be said about the relation between justification by faith and the sense of wholeness, the interconnectedness of things, because we experience justification as a personal event. Justification occurs when the individual self entrusts itself to God. There is no self-entrustment by proxy or by a group. That much is clear. What is not so clear is how this irreducibly personal act is related to the interconnectedness of all things. Actually, they are intimately related, once we remember that the self entrusts itself to God on a basis of the gospel, the good news of what God is up to in Jesus Christ. We can begin to see the relation if we recall that justification means rectification, the making right of relationships. As we shall see in a few moments, the rectification of the individual's relation to God is of a piece with the rectification of all relationships which God has undertaken in Christ. Consequently, the experience of being justified, of having one's relation to God rectified by faith opens out onto the rectification of all things.

If this is true, then rediscovering the power of justification does two things—it liberates the minister, like every believer, from compulsions to create one's own life, and it opens the window to see the interconnectedness of the personal redemption and that of the world.

Second, Paul's insight into the gospel can free us from the tyranny of a false choice between obligation and freedom. To oppose obligation and its structures of accountability in the name of the freedom of the Spirit is the road to disaster. Because finally it rests on the gnostic and Manicheean denial of body, history, and world in the name of a self or soul that is authentic only when freed from every constraint which makes us members of the human family. Let me be candid without being harsh. The ministry, like much of our culture, suffers from a distorted view of the freedom conferred by the Spirit—namely, a spurious emancipation from structures of accountability, from those rudimentary obligations to one another that make life human and humane. In the name of unquestioned spiritual freedom for the self, some ministers abandon family obligations, manipulate the dynamics of sexuality, and regard parishes and institutions as entities which must not be permitted to exercise any claims on the free self. Because freedom and obligation cannot be conceived to be co-extensive, there arises a cleavage between the private life where one insists on being free and the professional life with its obligations. But what Paul opens up is the promise of a deeper integrity, because when the relation to God is rectified by trust, the freedom conferred by the Spirit transforms the relation to obligations as well. What Paul points us toward is freedom from the compulsion to live without obligation in order to be free, and the freedom from the pressure to escape accountability and elemental personal morality in order to become authentic. From Paul's angle what law is all about, namely right relationships between persons and between persons and institutions as well as between institutions, can be affirmed because these relationships need no longer be manipulated in order to establish ourselves.

According to Paul, "the just requirement of the law" can be fulfilled precisely by those whom the Spirit frees from the perverting influence of the flesh, including a fleshly understanding of both human freedom and the divine Spirit. The freedom of the Spirit does not create autonomous, middle-class selves hell-bent on self-fulfillment but makes us free for comnunity and creation, both of which entail obligations. That too can be good news.

B. Next, Paul exposes the inseparability of life and thought, for in the fifth and sixth verses of our chapter he writes that "those who live according to the flesh set their minds on the things of the flesh, but those who live according to the Spirit set their minds on the things of the Spirit. To set the mind on the flesh is death, but to set the mind on the Spirit is life and peace." We have already seen that for Paul "flesh" is not simply the physical and the phenomenal as such, but the physical and the phenomenal when it becomes a domain of power exerting a determinative influence. This is why Paul writes of living or existing "according to" it, in conformity with it. Elsewhere in Romans he writes of becoming a slave of whatever one obeys. Moreover, "flesh" is not simply a specifiable thing; if it were, it could be placed off-limits and avoided. Rather, it is a structure of reality—more precisely, a perverted and perverting reality-structure. By contrast, "Spirit" is a life-giving structure of reality also laden with determining power. Spirit can be distinguished formally but not experientially from that field of force which Paul calls "Christ" (so that he can write now of being "in the Spirit" and now of being "in Christ"). Each of these contrasting domains has its own coherence, here expressed as the inseparability of existence and thought.

Actually, the coherence of life and thought involves more than thought. Paul is not writing of sheer cognition or intellection. The word he uses (*phronein*, *phronēma*) means "mind-set," "be disposed toward," and even "take the side of." Perhaps we can paraphrase the point: "Those who live according to flesh or according to Spirit orient their thinking toward the things of flesh or Spirit." What is normative for life becomes normative also for thought. What Paul said briefly, and almost in passing, has in our time been documented and analyzed by the disciplines of the sociology of knowledge, rooted in Marx and developed by Mannheim, on the one hand, and by Freud and his followers on the other. It would be illuminating to probe and compare the sociology and the psychology of knowledge with Paul, but I will leave that for somebody's dissertation. Here it suffices to note that Paul sees both the continuity of life and thought, and the primacy of existence for thought or mind-set because he sees that what one lives by shapes what one thinks about and how one does it.

Paul's intent here is not to explore clinically or diagnostically the various attempts to have it some other way, as he does in 1 Corinthians where he exposes the fact that the Corinthians actually construe the Spirit in a very fleshly way. Here it is the inherent logic of the alternatives that is in view because he wants to show certain consequences of moving from one domain to the other. That is, he assumes the inseparability of life and mind-set and construes this inseparability as both warning and promise. We recall that in 2 Corinthians 5 Paul writes analogously of knowing according to the flesh, and implies that there is another knowing which is in accord with the new creation. There it becomes clear that what new creation brings is not primarily new things to know, new objects of knowledge and thought (revealed concepts) but a new way of regarding, knowing, and thinking about realities already experienced. This is congruent with what was said earlier about the holy—it is not a special object alongside the profane but the perceived wholeness of things which stands over against our fragmentation. Coming back to our passage in Romans 8, this implies that life according to the Spirit, the Holy and hallowing Spirit, will also lead us to discern the wholeness of things, the interconnectedness of all existence because the One is present as power.

If Paul is on target, then ministry ought to manifest more coherence, more integrity of life and thought. The secularization of life and ministry which was noted earlier means that we live according to the flesh and still try to have a mind set according to the Spirit, or that we try to make space for special spiritual things in the jumbled room where we really live. Above all, if Paul is right, there is no validity in any spirituality which is really fleshly and utilitarian; that is, it is a self-distructing contradiction to learn how to pray or meditate in order to be more effective.

Such an approach is on the same spectrum as invitations to learn how to pray your fat away. The coherence of life and thought also implies that there is no true spirituality, or life according to the Spirit, which ignores the life of the mind, and plain hard thinking about reality. The spirituality of the ministry cannot be renewed by turning away from clear theological thinking, and there is no spiritual discipline that is not at the same time intellectual and moral discipline. Nor can the work of ministry be done in a bifurcated way, as when a preacher sets aside virtually everything learned about the biblical text in order to hear directly the word of the Lord from the same page. By such a practice ministers actually secularize the ministry in the name of spirituality. There is, of course, no so-called " spiritual exegesis" alongside ordinary exegesis, but there is a spiritual discernment "in, with, and under" exegesis.

C. The third passage concerns what Paul calls "the things of the Spirit." What are these? They are not another layer of reality, a layer of spiritual ideas in the Platonic sense. Rather, they are things derived from, dependent on, and consequences of the Spirit. Remarkably, Paul goes on to write that the Spirit activates and exposes the interconnectedness of all things. Living according to the Spirit does not divert attention from the world but directs us to our solidarity with the world just as much as it manifests our inseparability from God.

That the Spirit manifests and confirms an inseparable relation to God is clear in vv. 14 through 17: "For all who are led by the Spirit of God are sons of God.[2] . . . When we cry 'Abba! Father!' it is the Spirit himself bearing witness with our spirit that we are children of God and if children, then heirs, heirs of God and fellow heirs with Christ . . ." So too in the paragraph that begins with v. 26, Paul writes, "likewise the Spirit helps us in our weakness; for we do not know how to pray as we ought, but the Spirit intercedes for us with sighs too deep for words. And he who searches the human hearts knows what is the mind of the Spirit, because the Spirit intercedes for the saints according to the will of God." The inability to pray properly is not something that disciplined spirituality overcomes, but rather something that is acknowledged as part of the human condition. Indeed, living according to the Spirit is precisely what discloses the fact that we do not know what or how to pray as we ought. Paul implies that experts in true prayer can be found only among those who do not live according to the Spirit. This inability to pray rightly, however, is no more an obstacle to the relation to God than are sin or doubt, for the heart of the gospel is that it is not we who achieve a right relation to God but God who establishes a right relation to us. What Paul is saying here is nothing other than the doxological equivalent of justification by faith. It would be a travesty of the first order if justification meant that we were put in right relation to God so that now we could take into our own hands once again, only more successfully, the relation to God in prayer itself.

Even more unexpected, perhaps, is Paul's insistence that life according to the Spirit does not distance us from the fallen and unredeemed creation but intensifies the awareness of solidarity with it. He writes that not only has creation "been groaning in travail together until now, but we ourselves, who have the first-fruits of the Spirit, groan inwardly as we wait for adoption as sons, the redemption of our bodies." The body is part of creation which, Paul says, was subjected to futility but will be liberated from bondage to decay and share in the glorious liberty of the children of

---

2. We ought not make the masculinity of this language more important than it is for Paul, who abandons it in the next breath.

God. Living in accord with the Spirit clarifies and sharpens the "not yet" of redemption just as the earliest dawning makes us aware that the sun has not yet fully risen, even though the end of night is at hand. We may put it this way: the experience of the Spirit is the pledge to the person of the final redemption of the body, and the existence of Spirit-experiencing Christians is a pledge to the creation of its final redemption. Nowhere else in Paul does personal religious experience of the most intimate sort appear to be more clearly interconnected with the whole of creation than here. As noted before, here only the language of myth allows Paul to say what must be said.

To set one's mind, to focus one's thinking on the things of the Spirit is to begin to see the connecting tissues that give wholeness and power to the gospel. Earlier, in v. 11, Paul had written that "if the Spirit of him who raised Jesus from the dead dwells in you, he who raised Christ Jesus from the dead will give life to your mortal bodies also through his Spirit which dwells in you." It is all of a piece. The God who raised Jesus from the land of the dead sends the Spirit as a permanent resident in the self who trusts this God; this resident presence will transform the self as was Jesus; the God who raised Jesus and who will redeem the mortal body-self will redeem the mortal creation. in the meanwhile, to live by the Spirit is not simply to hold a victory party before the victory is complete; it is also to live by that life-giving power in such a way that one shares without anxiety the groaning of the unredeemed world.

Would not our attitude toward the not-redeemed creation be changed if we claimed Paul's vision as our own? Would we not discover that the gospel is much more than a fantastic story about what happened to Jesus one weekend long ago? Would we not forge a new attitude toward our own hurts and sufferings if we began seeing them as the inevitable signs of the "not yet" of redemption instead of regarding them as things we don't deserve and which therefore become the occasion for us to question the truth or value of the gospel itself? When suffering came to this apostle, at any rate, it appears not to have occurred to him to say, "I am suffering; therefore the gospel must be wrong," or to infer, "I am suffering, so there is no advantage to being in Christ; I would be just as well off as a Pharisee, maybe better"; or to reason, "I am suffering, therefore God has it in for me or is getting back at me." Nor does the question arise, "Compared with Peter and Barnabas, am I getting more than my fair share of suffering?" The comparison he does make in our chapter is between suffering now and redemption then (what he calls "the glory

PART 4: A WORD FOR BEARERS OF THE WORD

that is to be revealed to us"), and he dares to declare that the present is not worth comparing with the future. No cost-effectiveness formula for Paul. According to Paul's logic, the hurting ones touched by redemption are the ministers among the hurting destined for redemption. Ministry is not done by the isolated, the insulated, or those exempted from suffering which characterizes creation, but by those whom the Spirit makes children of God who know that their own redemption is not complete, and so is really a pledge, until all creation is liberated from death and rectified as well.

D. In the fourth passage, the concluding paragraph, Paul holds before us the interconnectedness of two things which we often play off against each other—vulnerability and vindication. Vulnerability pervades the passage, which begins with the imagery of the courtroom: who will bring any charge against God's elect? Who will condemn? Then the images of vulnerability shift to experiences which climax in death: tribulation, distress, persecution, famine, nakedness, peril, sword. A quotation from Psalm 44 caps it off: "For thy sake we are being killed all the day long; we are regarded as sheep to be slaughtered." In the peroration we have a third cycle of threats, this time cosmic forces: death, life, angels, principalities, the present, the future, powers, height and depth—against none of these is there natural (or supernatural) immunity. At the same time, the paragraph that immediately precedes announces a vulnerability that combines a Stoic view of, providence, according to which God works everything out for good, and a biblical view according to which God vindicates the elect in the face of adversity: Those whom God foreknew God predestined, and the predestined are called and the called are justified, and the justified are glorified. Then when Paul moves into our paragraph, it turns out that he mentions the threats to which one is vulnerable only to reject them. Since God justifies (here understood as vindicates), no accusation can stand; since the one who intercedes for us is the Christ whom God vindicated by resurrection, Christ will not condemn us either. So none of the dangers mentioned can really do us in, because nothing and no one in all creation can separate us from God's love in Christ. In fact, he declares flatly that " in all these things we are more than conquerors through him who loved us."

Our main problem is the disparity between his resounding affirmation and what we can believe. Several decades ago, many ministers read with appreciation the book bearing the title, *Your God Is too Small*. Today, I suspect, that many of us who read the concluding paragraphs of

Romans would want someone to give us a copy of *Your God Is too Great*. The change in outlook does not necessarily reveal greater wisdom, but it does disclose a different sensibility. Many, doubtless, are the factors that produced this shift, but surely prominent among them is a growing sense of powerlessness in the face of apparently intractable problems, including precisely the ones Paul mentions—persecution, famine, poverty, and war—hot or cold. Indeed our list is even longer than Paul's, for we would add the tyranny of governmental bureaucracy, the relentless ravaging of the earth with its air and water, racism, and crime in places high and low. The vision of the Great Society from which poverty would be banished and in which justice would be established elicits now a range of responses, few of which are affirming. No, Paul, we think that in all these things we are less than conquerors, little more than Dutch boys with their f ingers in the dikes, holding back for a moment the deluge. Not conquering but "coping" is our aim; not surmounting but surviving is the goal. Apart from the once-born optimists among us, what a growing cadre of ministers look forward to is not the triumph of cause after cause but trench warfare. We are not girding up our loins but digging in our heels. This depression that appears to be settling upon some of us too can be a sign of secularization, a loss of the sense of the reality and freedom of God, for it reduces the capacity of God to what seems possible for us to achieve.

One can say, of course, that the swing from a manic to a depressive state was inevitable precisely because the whole sense of the future was based on anthropology instead of being grounded in christology and theology—that is, it was rooted more in a view of the human capacity than in an understanding of the divine freedom, a freedom that in the Bible includes the capacity to tear down as well as build up and is not generally reducible to the logarithmic function of human capacity to achieve goals.

Over against our current mood, complicated somewhat by the resolute confidence of Marxist Christians, we hear the words of Romans 8 again, and this time we notice that the only note of triumphalism is in v. 37 that has the "more than conquerors" phrase, and this goes on to qualify the victory as coming "through him who loves us"—namely God. It is our utilitarian mentality that gets in the way here, for according to this mindset what we call "God" is our means of triumph, our ultimate weapon as we battle to redeem creation. But when Paul alludes to God as "the one who loved us" he is making a series of cross-references, all of which refer to God's sending the Son into the pit of death and to God's vindicating him by resurrection. This is the God who exposes the weakness of power and whose own power is hidden in weakness without being absent from it. As Romans 9–11 will claim, this God is as truly at work in Pharoah as in Moses, in breaking off one olive branch as in grafting another one. Consequently, when Paul writes of being "more than conquerors through him who loved us," he is drawing the consequences for human life of who he sees God to be. Nowhere does he say that persecution, famine, nakedness, peril or sword will be defeated if only we keep at it long enough, for Paul does not make his view of God rest finally on a doctrine of progress. It rests instead on the meaning of Christ, here formulated to say "He who did not spare his own Son, but gave him up for us all—will he not also give us all things with him?" In other words, a God who can do what was done in Christ is able to complete the task, regardless of whether we ourselves "win, lose, or draw." In the meantime, nothing we experience, including the triumphs we fail to experience, can "separate us from the love of God in Christ Jesus our Lord."

What allows Paul to hold together vulnerability and vindication is not simply the capacity of his dialectical mind but the paradoxical event of Jesus Christ. He is the basis of our hope, and as Paul says earlier in this chapter, "in this hope we are saved."

III

Is there good news for ministers? Yes. I am convinced that there is—but only if one is willing to attend to texts like Romans 8, if one is willing to listen carefully, to converse openly with it, and to be instructed—that is, modified—by it. Anything less is a quick fix.

13

The Fear of the Lord Is the Beginning of Knowledge (Proverbs 1:7)

It is fitting that we begin here—in Marquand Chapel. In a few minutes something else will begin—the annual Talkathon when we lay end to end more welcomes, more presentations, more speeches, more capsules of information than you will ever encounter at this School again. Orientation is important; we are glad you are here, and we want to integrate into our community each entering student, and we want to do so warmly, and as efficiently as possible. It is important that our beginning is right. So we begin our beginning right here, orienting ourselves to God before we orient you to the ways of this institution.

The word for the day—our text—is also about beginning: "The fear of the Lord is the beginning of knowledge" (Prov 1:7). This declaration from the Book of Proverbs joins together what we often drive apart and hold apart—commitment and critical inquiry. So at the beginning this old saying gives us pause, and invites us to begin in a different mode.

I

The concern of the proverb is ours as well—knowledge. To be sure, it is not our only concern, and it might not even be our primary one. All sorts of reasons and motives have brought us together. Some of us are interested in finding and focusing a clear professional goal, something that will be our own within that vague field called "ministry." Others of us think that our professional identities are clear enough; what we seek is strategies for saving the world from one of its possible forms of disaster, so that our quest for knowledge becomes a shopping trip for weaponry with which to battle the hosts of darkness. Some of us came in search of a vital faith, to test whether this thing called "the Christian faith" makes enough sense and has enough power for us to claim it for ourselves. Others of us are here not so much because the Lord called us as because somebody thought we would "make a good minister." Be assured that whatever motive brought you here, you are welcome. Be also assured that this place values knowledge. In fact you would not have chosen a university divinity school had you not cherished knowledge also. And you have come to the right place—a divinity school in a university which proclaims on its emblem *lux et veritas*, for light and truth are what we are about.

The desire for knowledge should not be taken for granted. Not in our time. Not with regard to the ministry either. In some ears the phrase "a learned ministry" sounds quaint, and in others it sounds elitist. Moreover, we live in a time when the feelings are paramount, when how a person feels about something is regarded as far more important than how one thinks about it or knows about it. From such a standpoint it is but a short step to regard our prejudices as more important than any knowledge which might disturb them. So the School's valuing of knowledge has a certain edge to it, a measure of deliberate antithesis to a widespread attitude.

In this place, the knowledge we seek to share is the wisdom of the Christian communities and their traditions. This is richer than any of us can experience directly. It is a legacy of experience distilled into teachings, formalized into structures, and built into values more diverse than most of us can imagine without instruction and disciplined inquiry. The Bible alone puts us in touch with the hopes and agonies of people who in more than a dozen centuries fell to depths of despair and soared to heights of enthusiasm which put to shame the narcissistic preoccupations that bedevil many of us. The experience of the church, now bold in its fidelity, now arrogant in its folly, offers ample precedent for considering the shape of our own discipleship. The experience of the church, whether in developing doctrines or in forging life-styles, reminds us again and again that today's wisdom is denounced as folly by the next generation. The library is a veritable mausoleum of "new theologies," all of which promised to overcome the follies of the past. The ministries of the church, and the slogans that promote them today, will seem quaint and narrow tomorrow. One of the things that characterizes the divinity school is a persistent attention to historical understanding, including the understanding of understanding. This is not because we are floorboarding it into the future with our gaze fixed on the rearview mirror. We take seriously our legacy because we are convinced that by knowing it well and engaging it critically we make it possible for knowledge to mature into wisdom. No school, no curriculum devised by the faculty, and no program of study put together by the students can guarantee that knowledge will ripen into wisdom or that foolishness will atrophy. What the knowledge we seek together can do is to keep us humble as we realize that there are more questions than answers, and that what is finally required of us is fidelity to what we do know in the presence of so much that we do not know. This is why the beginning is the fear of the Lord.

II

Actually, we do not like this proverb: "The fear of the Lord" can give us all kinds of problems, beginning with the word "Lord" itself. For some of us it is far too masculine a way of referring to God. Only a neuter deity will do. For others, "Lord" is far too power-oriented. We are prepared to speak of God as the lover and suggester but not as one who has sovereign authority, because it is our power that concerns us most. Others resist the whole idea of fear in relation to God. Such a notion is too primitive, too unworthy of God or ourselves. Our text, of course, does not advocate a relation to God based on terror. What it has in view is awe, a deep awareness that God's ways are not ours, that the word "God" refers to a mystery we acknowledge but cannot master, but which surrounds us and confounds us just as much as it supports and sustains us. All our knowledge has its beginning and its end in this insight. No matter how much we come to know, if we miss this we will miss it all.

But still we are suspicious of our proverb, and for opposite reasons—reasons far more profound than the simplistic objection to either the word "Lord" or the word "fear." Some of us are suspicious of knowledge because it might dissipate vital faith, and some of us are suspicious of "the fear of the Lord" because it might hamper the pursuit of knowledge.

That the fear of the Lord has impeded free critical inquiry is abundantly clear. Knowledge of the church's track record in this matter does make one ashamed. The story of Galileo has been repeated far too often. The right of free critical inquiry into Scripture cannot be taken for granted everywhere even today, as Missouri Synod Lutherans, Seventh-Day Adventists, and in some quarters Southern Baptists can testify. Only a few months ago, a nearby Evangelical seminary accepted the resignation of a New Testament professor whose historical conclusions about Jesus and John the Baptist were judged incompatible with a doctrinal view of Scripture. Again and again, Christians devout and sincere have concluded that only that knowledge is safe which is controlled by the fear of the Lord, translated into doctrine; they have decided that the free pursuit of knowledge—whether about the Bible or Christ or the church—will finally dissipate religious faith. And they have cited case after case when this in fact occurred. So some parts of the Christian family have fought rear-guard engagements against free inquiry, and have insisted that one cannot have both fidelity to God and free critical pursuit of knowledge. This is what the second career student, who had been a lay preacher, meant when he told me one day, "I could preach a whole lot more fervently before I knew so much about the Bible."

So those who have a deep commitment to the religious truth they inherited are suspicious of free inquiry, and those who take free inquiry for granted are suspicious of the heavy hand of dogma. Neither is comfortable with our text.

And for the same reason—both have the same faulty understanding of faith and knowledge. What binds these two suspicions together is the shared notion that faith and knowledge are essentially two forms of the same thing. Such a view can lead either to a conviction that knowledge is better than faith and so replaces it, or to the assumption that faith is better than knowledge and so fulfills it. Both invite disappointment. The person who thinks that knowledge is better than faith will inevitably conclude that the more one knows the less need for faith—as if faith were a matter of affirming things before we know them. The person who thinks that faith is better than knowledge will assume that knowledge leads to faith, that the more that is known the stronger the faith, because faith is perfected knowledge. Along this path disappointment is certain. The disappointment was confessed to me by an undergraduate at Wellesley, who said she took the seminar in the Quest for the Historical Jesus thinking that if only she knew more she could believe more easily, but it didn't turn out that way at all.

THE FEAR OF THE LORD IS THE BEGINNING OF KNOWLEDGE

III

When our text uses the phrase "the fear of the Lord" it is not referring to beliefs about God, to ideas about God, to doctrines; it is not speaking about theology at all. It is talking about the relationship to God. What it has in view is respect for the integrity of God as the reality with which we have to do. What it sees is the need to acknowledge that this reality must not be domesticated into a cosmic pal nor manipulated into a warrant for what we want to do, not even the good things we want to do. Our text is about respect for the otherness of God, the transcendence of God. Even more, it does not urge us to believe that God is transcendent, but to relate to God as a transcendent reality.

Getting this distinction clear and appropriating it is the most important part of orientation to a course of study in a divinity school, because the knowledge we seek and seek to share will surely challenge the ideas of God which we bring to our work. Unless this distinction is clear, it will be all too easy to conclude that whatever challenges our beliefs about God threatens our relation to God. To be sure, the ideas we have about God inform the way we relate to God; but it is one thing to trust our ideas about God and another thing to trust God.

If there is fear of the Lord in this sense, if we distinguish trusting our ideas of God from trusting God, then we are free to seek knowledge wherever it can be found. Then the pursuit of knowledge, be it knowledge of the Bible or of doctrine or of sociology or of the church, will not threaten the relation to God even when it is transformed because it will be enlarged. There is no need to fear what the faculty will teach or what several years at Yale Divinity School will do to your faith. Be assured that ideas will be confronted with other ideas; convictions will be relativized by the convictions of others; cherished values will be spurned and things you regarded as minor will be held up as decisive. And you will be changed in the process; and sometimes with pain. But the reality and mystery we call "God" is not being dismembered but only certain ideas about God. You are truly free to seek knowledge and its consequences if your quest begins with the fear of the Lord, if you understand from the outset that the God to whom our language and our symbols point is also free and is not the prisoner of any doctrine, any social program, or any view of justice and peace. And a free God is not intimidated by our doubts nor made anxious by our convictions. Our theologies may dissolve and our values be transformed, but God remains God.

PART 4: A WORD FOR BEARERS OF THE WORD

To know this, to respect the Godhood of God, and to entrust oneself to God is to be truly oriented to the acquisition of knowledge about God and about God's world. In these days you will be told many things that you should not forget. But the one thing you should remember is that "the fear of the Lord is the beginning of knowledge."

PART 5

The Word Borne

The book ends with four sermons, preached in significantly diverse pulpits but during the same stressful decade when things long held together were coming apart, and when urged alternatives promised more than they delivered. Then, perhaps more than even now, Bible-rooted sermons had to be theologically serious, not merely earnest.

The first sermon in this set was preached at the joint meeting of the Divine Word Seminary's faculty at Tagaytay, Philippines, and the faculty of Union Theological Seminary, south of Manila, where I was Visiting Professor of New Testament in the Spring semester, 1971. The churches, like Philippine society, were torn by conflicts that soon would be suppressed by martial law.

The second piece is a Palm Sunday sermon preached in varying forms in churches in Alabama, Georgia, and Tennessee between 1962 and 1977. The third and fourth are Advent sermons. One version of the third was preached at Battell Chapel at Yale in 1979; another version a year later in the First Congregational Church in Greenwich, Connecticut. The fourth was delivered to colleagues and students at Vanderbilt Divinity School in 1968. The date probably suffices to suggest the atmosphere in which this sermon was preached and heard.

INTRODUCTION TO PART 5

Be that as it may, Isaiah's word of hope summons also us to lean into the future.

14

Summoned to Christian Unity
(Ephesians 4:7–16)

These are strange times in which to celebrate the drive toward Christian unity. Let me mention just two reasons this appears to be the case. First, the ecumenical movement has generally had an institutional form. Thus the World Council of Churches, for example, has insisted that it is not a conglomerate of Christians but a council of churches; and when Protestants were invited to attend Vatican II it was representatives of churches who were sent. But it is just this official, establishment-oriented cast of ecumenism that has brought it to a certain impasse, for especially among the young it is no longer self-evident that any form of the institutional church that we know has a future. What a former colleague once said about COCU, the effort to amalgamate nine or so American denominations, the disenchanted might also say of institutional ecumenism—that it was an effort to re-arrange the deck chairs on the Titanic. As we rejoice and worship with one another, we ought not to ignore this ironic element in the situation.

Second, these are strange times in which to celebrate Christian unity because Christians are not only finding one another but are being driven apart as well. In the States, as elsewhere, churches are divided, often bitterly, over involvement in social and political affairs, and many a communion finds itself virtually split. During my recent brief stop in Japan, I was informed that this cleavage has become so bitter that for several years no regional synod or national assembly could be held at all, for the gathering would explode. In addition, everywhere the power of nationalism is asserting itself, threatening to turn the world-wide church into a loose confederation of national cults. I suspect that a major issue in our future will be the tension between the drive for thorough Christian unity on the one hand, and the drive for churchly participation in nationalist, and hence separatist, surges everywhere. How, then, can we celebrate Christian unity on this volcano?[1]

Our text has a word for us.

> But each of us was given grace according to the measure of Christ's gift. Therefore it is said,
> "When he ascended on high he made captivity itself a captive; he gave gifts to his people."
> (When it says, "He ascended," what does it mean but that he had also descended into the lower parts of the earth? He who descended is the same one who ascended far above all the heavens, so that he might fill all things.) The gifts he gave were that some would be apostles, some prophets, some evangelists, some pastors and teachers, to equip the saints for the work of ministry, for building up the body of Christ, until all of us come to the unity of the faith and of the knowledge of the Son of God, to maturity, to the measure of the full stature of Christ. We must no longer be children, tossed to and fro and blown about by every wind of doctrine, by people's trickery, by their craftiness in deceitful scheming. But speaking the truth in love, we must grow up in every way into him who is the head, into Christ, from whom the whole body, joined and knit together by every ligament with which it is equipped, as each part is working proprly, promotes the body's growth in building itself up in love.

This is a strange text, first quite remote from us. The author, whoever may have been, is concerned for the unity of the church in the face of the tension beween Jew and Greek. In any case, my aim is not to help us listen in on *that* problem then, but to help us all to listen to what the text can say to us now.

Let us not be put off by the use of Psalm 68, which the author articulates into his situation in such a strange way. Let us rather observe his aim—to insist that the risen Lord gave diverse gifts to his church: apostles, prophets, evangelists, pastors, teachers. In contrast with Paul himself, his disciple does not speak of capacities for leadership, of charismata, but of church offices. That is, he speaks of institutional leadership roles as gifts of the Lord. We are not happy about this, suspicious as we have become

---

1. "Volcano" here is both a metaphor and a reference to the location of the Divine Word Seminary.

about institutions and their establishment-minded leaders. Nonetheless, we should not read the Bible simply to find those precious passages that confirm what we already know, but must read precisely those parts that cut across the trajectory of our inclinations. What, then, do we do with our text?

We read a little farther and learn that these institutional gifts are given for the equipping of the saints, for the work of service, for the building up of the body of Christ. Here is the decisive point: these offices must equip the whole church for its mission in the world. We do not hear this text rightly so long as we merely acknowledge it as a pious idea or a high ideal. We hear it rightly only as a summons to the whole Christian brotherhood, as a call to insist that its leaders, whatever they be called or however they be ordained and garbed, respond rightly to what is said here.

Let me be concrete. This text is given to the whole church, precisely to the saints who are the body of Christ. This means that the whole Christian community is held accountable for its obedience to what is said here. The real significance of Christian unity does not lie in the fact that a leader of one church will be free to preach in the pulpit of another, nor in the fact that we occasionally get together to nurture fraternal feelings, important as this is in view of the past. Rather, the real power of Christian ecumenism emerges when Christians find each other, and when they find each other to be faithful brothers and not simply congenial exceptions to their prejudices. Moreover, having found each other, they draw strength from one another and from their common Lord, and so ask of their respective leaders better equipping of the saints, more careful attention to the task of ministry, and less concern for preserving the power of the churches. To say it bluntly, the time is past when we can apply the trickle-down theory of economic wealth to the cause of Christian unity, and to the life of the church in the world, and so assume that once people at the top get together the nectar of Christian unity will trickle down to parched Christians at the bottom of the pyramid. The time is at hand for Christians who find one another to rejuvenate the structures above them. Just as our text does not sanctify wholesale alienation from institutional leadership, so it calls us to see that the church institutions we know function for the sake of mission. Because the current suspicion of institutions is not a peculiarity of one group but is a phenomenon we all know, each in his own way, we are not permitted to find one another and then merely pool our complaints. You know the kind of thing: "Now let me tell you one about *my* bishop." Rather, in finding each other, we also find strength to insist that the structures within which we labor truly serve the mission of the church, and so the whole can be renewed.

But our text has more to offer, for it says what is to happen when the church knows its task and functions rightly to fulfill it. It speaks of being no longer children, tossed back and forth and carried this way and that by every wind of doctrine, by the cunning and craftiness of men. How does this text accost us today?

It asserts that the risen Christ gives diverse gifts and that the proper use of this diversity is an effective alternative to being pulled this way and that. We know a good deal about the lures of contradictory ideologies, for in our time the doctrines that divide us are not creedal but ideological. What church and what Christian does not feel himself pulled this way and that, one day called to defend the tradition against new forms of gnosticism and on the next pullled into an ideological stance in support of a violent revolution or a nationalism? Let me be clear. I find nationalism no less dangerous when it is American. Who among us has remained untouched by the polarization that causes us to disdain whoever is not with us at whatever pole we may be at the time? Do we not face a new Donatism that threatens to set minimum requirements for those with whom we are willing to share the name "Christian"?

But just here our text can redeem us from the ideological morasse, for it suggests that a pluralistic church can avoid being polarized, that a diversified brotherhood can cope with the multiple calls of ideologies. In the cause of Christian unity more is at stake than simply uniting Christians. Rather when we accept one another with our diverse gifts and diverse histories, we will become a genuinely pluralistic community. If we become this, we shall also learn how to accept those who differ from us in political and economic judgments. A pluralistic church, where we know we are one in the Lord, can save us from being torn apart and save the church from being subverted into a political party on the right or on the left in the name of Christ. Furthermomre, it could well be that only a pluralistic world-wide church is capable of dealing with those blatant forms of nationalism that pervert constructive nation-building into xenophobic Christian zealotism. Surely we shall not allow our several nationalisms to turn the church into a mere ecclesiastical replica of an impotent UN based on national boundaries. Is it not the case that when we are one in Christ are we truly free to build our nations in community?

And so, if we have heard our text aright, it will set us on our feet to march together as brothers in Christ who are not content until the structures of our churches truly facilitate and abet the mission that Christ gave us, and then we will not get in the way of that mission. Our text can put our hands to the task of developing as quickly as possible a truly pluralistic church not beholden to any ideology. In this way we can also do what the conclusion of our text bids us do—speak the truth in love, that is, speak it to one another candidly, and forthrightly to a fractured world. Amen.

15

King Jesus?

> The next day a great crowd who had come t othe feast heard that Jesus was coming to Jerusalem. So they took a branches of palm trees and went out to meet him, crying,
> "Hosanna!
> Blessed be he who comes in the name of the Lord,
> even the King of Israel!" [Ps 118:14].
> And Jesus found a young ass and sat uon it; as it is written,
> "Fear not, daughter of Zion;
> behold, your king is coming,
> sitting on an ass's colt!" [Zech 9:9]
> His disciples did not understand this at first; but when Jesus was glorified, then they remembered that this had been written of him and had been done to him. The crowd that had been with him when he called Lazarus out of the tomb and raised him from the dead bore witness. The reason why the crowd went out to meet him was that they had heard he had done this sign. The Pharisees then said to one another, "You see that you can do nothing; look, the world has gone after him." (John 12:12–19)

Palm Sunday is one of the great festivals of the Christian church around the world. Palm Sunday celebrates the day when people welcomed Jesus to the Holy City. We sometimes call this event his "Triumphal Entry."

Christians enjoy Palm Sunday, for we see Jesus enter the city with shouts of acclamation from the crowds, and we regard the palms as symbols of the kind of response he deserves. We are tired of reading about how people misunderstood him and misrepresented him, how they opposed him and argued with him. At last, the response to the mission of

Jesus changes, even if but for a moment, and we can see something happen that should have happened long before. So we rejoice to see him ride into town like a hero on the Fourth of July. We like Palm Sunday because we'd like to make Jesus the marshall of the Rose Parade.

Our Evangelist, John, seems to suspect what we are thinking. Right in the middle of the short story, he sounds a warning. To be sure, what he actually writes reads like a straightforward description of the disciples who were there, who were part of the action. But in writing about those disciples, he is sounding a warning to later disciples who were not there but who are now reading the story. Remember John's comment? "His disciples did not understand this at first; but when Jesus was glorified, then they remembered that this had been written of him and had been done to him." In other words, those who were there did not understand what was happening until after Jesus' death and resurrection. That is when Jesus was glorified. The reason they did not understand it when it was happening is that they thought he was being glorified then and there, that the pomp and circumstance was his glorification. Not so, says John. Not until after Jesus was executed and raised did they understand that what happened on Palm Sunday was no glorification at all.

John's way of understanding Jesus' entry to Jerusalem is not the only way of understanding it, even in the New Testament. Here is one of those places where the four Gospels do not agree, and this is frustrating to the historian who wants to know exactly what happened. But each Gospel tells it differently. The main difference is that in the first three Gospels Jesus takes the initiative and sends two disciples into the village to fetch a colt on which to ride, and the crowd responds to the sight of Jesus riding on the colt. In John, however, it is Jesus who responds to what the crowd was doing. Each of the Gospels tells the story the way it does in order to highlight something, and what is highlighted is a facet of the gospel message that each writer wants to emphasize. So let's listen closely to what John wants us to hear.

John's warning pointed to what he wanted us to hear: What had been written about Jesus and what had been done to him, namely the action of the crowd. Part of what the crowd did was to quote a well-known psalm. From John's point of view, what the crowd said manifested the wrong understanding of the matter, for the right understanding came only after Easter. Only after Easter, says John, did the disciples remember that the Old Testament prophet Zechariah had written some lines about a king on an ass's colt. They remembered these lines when the real point of the event, and the larger story of which it was a part, came clear.

So we need to recall the larger story. The thread goes back into the previous chapter, where we find the story of how Jesus raised Lazarus from the dead. As John tells it, this incident set into motion the plot to get rid of Jesus. A week before Easter, Lazarus and his two sisters, Mary and Martha, had a dinner party for Jesus and his friends. And this event drew a crowd of onlookers who wanted to see Lazarus. He had become a tourist attraction. The next day was Palm Sunday. In other words, the crowd went out to greet Jesus with the words of Psalm 118 in their mouths and with palms in their hands because they heard that the man who raised Lazarus was coming to town. Anybody who can do that deserves a special welcome.

Indeed, this was a welcome for a king. Both what they said and what they did make this clear. What they did was to wave palm branches—which, by the way, are mentioned only in this Gospel. Palm branches were the symbols of the victories of kings. During the brief times when the Jews emancipated themselves from Rome, they struck their own coins and on them they put the palm branches. Everyone in those days knew that the palm was the sign of kingly triumph. What the crowd shouted showed that they greeted Jesus as a king. They quoted a line from the psalm, "Blessed is he who comes in the name of the Lord," and then added an interpretation, "the king of Israel." By shouting this at Jesus they were hailing him as king.

Any way you look at it, this was a remarkable thing to do. For one thing, Jesus was not the king. Indeed, there was no king, and that was part of the problem. Some years before, the territory around Jerusalem had been placed under direct Roman administration, and the man in charge was called "procurator." And the procurator was now in residence inside the city. His names was Pilatus. Under those circumstances, hailing somebody as a king was dangerous. It was an act of revolution.

This was also a remarkable welcome when you consider the man who received it. Jesus was not a king-type. Nonetheless, the theme of Jesus as king is important is John's Gospel. According to John, after Jesus fed the multitudes, people tried to make him king, but he refused and slipped away. A few days after the Palm Sunday event, Jesus will be executed as King of the Jews. What happened? Did Jesus change his mind and decide to become king afte rall? No way. John says that during his trial Jesus stood before Pilatus, who asked him point blank, "Are you the king of the Jews?" It was then that Jesu said, "My kingship is not of this world"—that is, not derived from this world, not nourished by it nor dependent on it. Jesus is the king who is not a king, the non-king who is really king. That is what our story is about, and that is what could not be understood at the time. The whole thing was so strange.

Remember the story! The crowd gives Jesus an enthusiastic reception that was fit for a king. Indeed, they called him king. Why not? anybody who can raise the dead cannot be defeated in battle. No casualty lists could hold him back. What a leader he would be! A liberating king who can work miracles! People always yearn for such a figure. The more bleak the political and economic situation, the greater the hope for a miracle-working leader. So they hail him as king. Maybe this time he'll accept it. But what did Jesus do? He went and found a donkey and rode into town on that. What an odd response! No wonder the meaning of it was hidden at the time. Indeed, John implies that the meaning is still hidden unless we see it his way.

Kings ride horses, not donkeys. What Jesus did was far more of a surprise than Jimmy Carter walking from the Capitol to the White House on Inauguration Day. To get the flavor of what Jesus did we must imagine a folk-hero arriving in New York, which has gotten up a ticker-tape-parade welcome for him; a shining limousine is waiting to carry the hero through the streets. Instead of getting into it, this hero finds an old pickup truck and rides up the street in that. That's the sort of thing Jesus did, says John. He found a common beast of burden, an animal every farmer had, and rode that into the city. That was his response to the acclamation, "King of Israel." You see, the way John tells it this is not at all the story of Jesus' triumphal entry but the story of how he rejected a triumphal entry.

When John saw the point, he saw that the king is indeed on an ass's colt. Jesus will be king, but he will be a different kind of king. The sovereignty of Jesus is different from the rule of the kings of the world. Not only is the man on the throne different, but the monarchy is different also.

On Palm Sunday it is still easy to miss the point. It is still easy to stand along the Jerusalem road like a tourist. Crowds from all over the world still gather on this day to watch the children walk the route that Jesus took, and tourists line the road to snap their pictures to show the folks back home. I recall seeing one man in a ten-gallon hat, loaded down with three cameras, doubtless for black and white, color slides, and movies—as well as camera gear and a tripod. He elbowed his way to the edge of the road to record it all. It was an impressive sight. So was Jesus on the donkey, amid the shouts and palms. We can see it clearly and miss it plainly. We can simply look at Jesus and never take a second thought about what his action means for ours. On the other hand, our story has the power to uncover the truth—the truth about the sort of king Jesus truly is. Jesus is the king who frees.

In the very next paragraph, John reports that Jesus said, "If anyone serves me he must follow me, and where I am there shall my servant be also." And this Jesus is not on horseback, nor in limousines, but on the donkey, in the pick-up. Those who follow he leads along the road where he disenchants us from illusions of grandeur of every sort. Along this road, each of us discovers where that liberation from illusions takes place.

There is one place where that liberation is especially important today, and it has to do with the central theme of our story—kingly power. Before the week was over, the high priests shouted something else about a king. When Pilatus was teasing the crowd with this himiliated Jesus by saying, "Here is your king!" they hurled back a shout with which they exposed themselves and condemned themselves: "We have no king but Caesar." Here is a horrible confession of ultimate allegiance to the state, to political order and power.

One reason Watergate was so hard for the soul and psyche of America is that we have spent the last thirty years saying, in one way or other, "We have no king but Caesar." We said it many times when we insisted that in the Cold War, we must not rock the boat, criticize the system, or tolerate dissent. We said it when we insisted that Christianity and uncritical patriotism go hand in hand. The stateside agony over Viet Nam brought all that to a head, and Watergate added the final touch. We looked to the state to provide us everything, and believed its pretensions and winked at its lies. In the name of national security we were prepared to tolerate anything. This was our way of saying, "We have no king but Caesar."

The story of Jesus can emancipate us from that blind loyalty to government that brought us into the recent crisis, and therefore into the present cynicism as well. The story of Jesus can do that by uncovering the truth about power and about our allegiance to power. It can do it by inviting us to welcome this sovereign on the donkey to be the real king. The only way to be free from the tyranny of having no king but Caesar is the welcome this Jesus as the final sovereign, to greet him not as a strange man making a foolish response to a great opportunity, but as the one who sees through the pretensions of power in every Pontius Pilate in any generation.

There is no salvation in simply observing Jesus. Salvation comes when we pick up our palms and greet him as our king on his terms, when this man and no other has the final say over our lives. And that is life eternal.

16

Are You the Coming One?
(Matthew 11:2–6)

> When John heard in prison what the Messiah was doing, he sent word by his disciples and said to him, "Are you the one who is to come, or are we to wait for another?" Jesus answered them, "Go and tell John what you hear and see: the blind receive their sight, the lame walk, the lepers are cleansed, the deaf hear, and the dead are raised, and the poor have good news brought to them. And blessed is anyone who takes no offense.

The question was right up front. Besides, it was well put—crystal clear and sharp as a rapier. Not an invitation to ramble on about one's thoughts, but as pointed a question as one might ask, "Are you the Coming One, or should we look for another?"

Where did it come from, this arrow that hummed right into the bullseye, and who sent it on its way? It came from the tortured heart of a political prisoner, from the mind of one whose uncompromising word about the sex life of the puppet king Herod enflamed the hatred of the new queen, Herodias. Herod had divorced his wife in order to marry his sister-in-law, a scheming bitch who finally found a way to silence the tongue of this forthright man who dared to tell the king, "It is not lawful for you to have your brother's wife." Some time before the head of this prophet was delivered on a platter during a late night revel, this austere man came to hear about another preacher, and what he heard both fascinated and disturbed him until he had to know whether he was the Coming One or not.

Before he was a prisoner, John had been a desert preacher. For reasons not altogether clear he renounced what we call civilization. Clothed in the shaggy skin of a camel and living off locusts and wild honey, he made the Jordan Valley his turf, that geological marvel that begins six hundred feet below sea level and then descends to the Dead Sea. Here, under the burning sun, he summoned his fellow Jews to righteousness and repentance; those who responded he baptised into the holy remnant. What made it all so urgent was the sense that the end was at hand. On that terrible day when God would call a halt to history, there was only one thing that would see you through—repentance and righteousness. On that terrible day, it would not be enough to be a member of the chosen people. "Do not say to yourselves, 'We have Abraham as our father!' For I tell you, God can make Jews from these stones." John also knew what the Coming One, God's agent, would do. He would sift his people the way the farmers sifted their grain by throwing it up into the air so the grain would fall and the chaff be blown away. So near is this judgment that John declared, "His winnowing fork is in his hand, and he will clear his threshing floor and gather his wheat into the granary but the chaff he will burn in unquenchable fire." Nothing less than a clean sweep will do. The vat that holds the grapes of wrath is full. For John, the Coming One would be God's agent through whom God will see to it that all persons got what they deserved.

And then he heard about his man from Galilee whom he had baptized, but who now was preaching the kingdom of God and had the reputation of a healer. From John's angle, Jesus had so much going for him—and yet he didn't seem to fit the hope. It was not curiosity that caused the question to be sent by couriers, but the pressing need to know whether in fact he was the Coming One on whom he counted, whether God's man of the end-time was actually here. If the Coming One is on the scene, John's own life-work would be vindicated; if not, if he must look for another, then he might have miscalculated. He had said that already the axe is cutting away at the root of the tree—but if he must wait for someone else, then maybe the axe was not at the root after all. So John sent his question: "Are you the Coming One, or shall we look for another?"

ARE YOU THE COMING ONE?

I

Now the curious thing is that the question John asked is also our question, especially so on the first Sunday in Advent when we celebrate the claim that the hope for the Coming One was fulfilled. And we ask it for much the same reason—we have our expectations of the Coming One, and we have heard about this Jesus, and the two don't match up. There may be even more pathos in our asking the question than there was in his, for we have seen so many more march by. Did not a German philosopher, Hegel, who talked much about the self-actualization of spirit, look out the window to see Napolean and conclude that he saw the world-soul riding by? A little more than a century later, did not a whole nation acclaim the Führer Prinzip and hail its Hitler as the Coming One who would make all things right and cleanse the earth of all things vile, including Jews? Have we not had our fill of messiahs, gurus, deliverers, instruments of divine righteousness, heroes, and saints of revolutions? How is it that we keep on looking for the Coming One? Are we really incurably utopians after all? Apparently so. Every four years we look for a Coming One to elect as father, king, redeemer, judge, as wise as Solomon, folksy as Lincoln, but oratorical as Churchill. The Coming One many desire in the White House is Clark Kent, who can emerge as Superman whenever needed.

As did John, so we want the Superman we look for to conform to our hopes and values, for only so can he confirm them to us. So it is natural that John's question to Jesus is ours as well, but Jesus keeps confounding our expectations. Are we alienated intellectuals, despising our culture like John repudiated his? Then we inspect Jesus to make sure he is alienated enough from his culture to be the Coming One for us. Do we hold romantic notions about the indestructible goodness of the poor? Then we look to see whether Jesus truly tilts to the poor. Are we convinced that the coming of God's righteousness means that everyone gets what is deserved, so that those who oppose us are done in while we are vindicated as those who have been righteous all along? Then we are curious to see how Jesus treats the opposition, and like John, we are disappointed. This Jesus does not meet our specifications. When he bids a healed leper to go show himself to the priest in order to be allowed to return to society, Jesus is not alienated enough. When he warns the poor against being concerned for food and drink, he does not idealize them sufficiently. When he eats with Pharisees as well as tax collectors and sinners, he seems to lack any moral standard at all. He is not consistent enough, not ideologically pure enough, not revolutionary enough, not this enough and not that enough. Shall we look for another?

But it is not only his apparent *in*consistencies that make us ask John's question, but above all his consistencies. He is incorrigbly committed to his people, Jews at that. He is relentless in his effort to bring the Kingdom to all sorts of persons. No one is exempt from his call to repentance—the turning of life Godward. He really does bypass political problems, matters of economy, restructuring a tax system. His life-work does not seem to be driven by resentment and hate but is propelled by faith and love. The more he emerges as consistent in his devotion to God, whom he dares to call Papa, the more we who are sophisticated find the question on our lips, Are the the Coming One? Is it really you who is the criterion of the future?

Either we are disappointed because he does not measure up to our standards, or we sense that his integrity transcends them so that we wish he were more realistic; either way, John's question is ours.

II

We are scarcely made more comfortable by his answer. Surely a forthright question deserves a forthright answer, an unequivocal yes or no. Surely John, of all people, deserved it.

Bur suppose he had replied with a resounding yes! That would have been the great derailment. Nothing short of disaster. For then he would have diverted attention from the coming of God's reign to his own claim. That would only have prompted the next question, how do you know you are the coming one? Then the discussion would be on familiar turf indeed, for we know how to take it from there. What are your criteria? How do you know your religious experience is more valid than that of the next? What proof can you give? And the more we succeed in getting him to respond to these questions, the more we would get him to justify himself, and the more this occurred the less he would be the Coming One we seek, for one who justifies himself to us cannot liberate us, for he would already have bought into our bondage.

So how does Jesus reply? "Go and tell John what you hear and see: the blind receive their sight and the lame walk, lepers are cleansed and the deaf hear, and the dead are raised up, and the poor have good news preached to them. And blessed is he who takes no offense at me." What kind of answer is that? As if John had not heard about these things, as if it were not reports of just such activities that caused him to ask the question in the first place. What does a string of miracles prove? What is going on in this answer?

Two things at least, One comes to light when we see how stylized the answer is. It resonates with those parts of the Old Testament that speak of the signs of coming deliverance. It is a clue, a hint that what is going on in the work of Jesus is fulfillment of expected redemption. But no more than a clue or a hint, for Jesus was not the only worker of wonders on the scene. The other thing that is going on is that Jesus quietly turns the question back on the questioner, in order to redeem him, not from uncertainty about Jesus' opinions about himself, but to redeem him from his own preconceptions about the Coming One. We do not know whether John got the point, but I do know that a Wellesley junior did. She admitted one day in an advanced course on Jesus and the Gospels, that she had signed up for it thinking that if she knew more information about Jesus it might be easier to believe, to trust him with her life. "But," she said, "the more I know, the sharper the question becomes." Precisely! Jesus' reply is nothing less than an invitation to faith, to self-entrustment, to risking one's self to discern that in all the ambiguity that surrounds this man, he is indeed the Coming One. That is how we are redeemed from bondage to our own specifications for a redeemer. That is how we are invited to embark on a life of faith and trust. Jesus' answer bids John—and us—to commit ourselves not on the basis of getting more pluses than minuses on our checklist, but by venturing our loyalty. That is how it has to be if a human being is to draw us to God and not simply to himself as the founder of a cult or movement. Here is the paradox: he who did not announce himself as the Coming One, as the messiah, is the one we call Messiah.

III

Why rehearse this at the beginning of Advent? Because Advent is not simply the beginning of the Christmas rush in church. It is the time when we celebrate the messianic hope that Jesus redefined. What we hope for is the fulfillment of what he was and what he did, for he is the criterion of our expectation. To call Jesus the Messiah is to be liberated from all the messianisms that continue to beckon us, whether from the left or from the right. To call Jesus the Messiah is to say no to salvation through politics. The hope that we celebrate in Advent is no longer the hope for a messianic leader; it is rather the hope for the completion of what he began—the sovereignty of love and justice that begins in the human heart when it is made right with God.

We rehearse all this at Advent for yet another reason—to remind ourselves that by calling Jesus the Messiah, we announce our own readiness to join his cause, to share his passion to make real the sovereignty of God among humankind. If we participate in public life, we do so in the name and spirit of this man, who trusted the power of love more than the power of force, who trusted the power of truth more than the power of propaganda, who trusted the kingdom of God to make its way in the world.

Those who celebrate Advent—the arrival of this man as the Coming One—are among the blessed who take no offense at him, for they not only ask John's question, but affirm Jesus' answer, and so have come through to the kingdom of God.

17

The Promise and the Hope
(Isaiah 40)

I presume it must be Providence that schedules chapel services in such a way that I, a candle-burning Baptist and high church Disciple, find myself once again in this pulpit during Advent. No other festival of the Christian year gathers up our yearnings for redemption and puts them into focus so well as does Advent, the season for celebrating the Promise of His coming. In a unique way, it is the festival of hope. But here is the rub. We sense that we are strangers to our own festival. In another day it may have been true that "hope springs eternal from the human breast," but is it really this way for us critics who know that there are at least two sides to everything? Moreover, in light of our actual circumstance in this place, marked as it is by uncertainty and unrest, who dares to speak of hope? Above all, what basis is there for reflecting together about the quality of our hope? One thing is clear—we do not celebrate the hodge-podge of hopes we have, even less our capacity for hoping. That would be a vain celebration of ourselves, and its symbol would be the bootstrap. Nor is there a future in arguing the case for hoping, or for the legitimacy of what we hope for, because cogent thought and rigorous logic cannot renew within us that flame that flickers now and again. Just as we cannot be talked out of hope, so we cannot be talked into it. Rather it is the Promise that we celebrate; it is the Word from the Holy One pledging himself to be for us that we must hear again if we are to find our hope renewed.

That great Advent text, Isaiah 40, can become such a renewal text if we attend to it carefully so that it finds its way to the living center where what we are takes shape. This text comes from the unnamed prophet of the Exile who accosted the dispirited Jews in Babylon with a vision of God and with a summons to a vocation of being a light to the nations. True, we are not POWs like his first readers, but we do find ourselves exiled from the Christendom our fathers knew, estranged from our inheritance, uncertain of ourselves and confused about the future. While it is true that history does not flow in parallel columns so that we can make facile comparisons, we have enough in common with that situation to make it possible for us to listen and to ponder the meaning of our time in light of this text. Instead of preaching a sermon "at" you, I want to reflect with you about the import of this great Advent chapter. Hearing the text together is more important than hearing another exhortation.

How I wish I were persuaded that the time for his opening lines was now!

> Comfort, comfort my people,
> > says your God.
> Speak tenderly to Jerusalem,
> > and cry to her
> that her warfare is ended,
> > that her iniquity is pardoned
> that she has received from the LORD's hand
> > double for all her sins.

Would that were the case! But I fear that the time for these lines is not yet, because the people of God are but at the beginning of the ordeal. Perhaps in our lifetimes these lines will come into their own, but not now. In the meantime, other lines do spring to life.

The next strophe comes home to us in a way that is nothing less than astringent, and we do not readily warm up to what it has to say:

> A voice cries:
> "In the wilderness prepare the way of the LORD,
> > make straight in the desert a highway for our God,
> Every valley shall be lifted up
> > and every mountain and hill be made low;
> the uneven ground shall become level,
> > and the rough places a plain.
> And the glory of the LORD shall be revealed
> > and all flesh shall see it together,
> > for the mouth of the Lord has spoken."

This summons puts us where we do not want to be—in the wilderness. Here is work to be done. Here there is no glory manifest but glory promised, here no epiphany of the divine makes us sure but the promise sets in motion the vocation of making things straight. Let me put it bluntly: to find our vocation in this wilderness is to go about our task in a time when one speaks of the absence of God, the eclipse of God, when the arrogant phrase "the death of God" is in the air. It is to take up our tasks on the basis of the promise that the glory of the Lord shall be revealed. We do not welcome this text. Are we not told that we are citizens of the city of man, the ever-more wondrous super-city inhabited by men priding themselves that they have "come of age," a habitation where the enigmas of man are all reduced to problems, then factored into manageable components? But it is mostly wilderness in the history of man. It is wilderness where rats prey on children and landlords on their parents, where bellies are swollen with famine and minds shrivelled with despair; it is the wilderness where the people perish because there is no vision even while hucksters peddle visions in living color. I need not report the inventory of this wilderness. I need only awaken the awareness that this is where we are, and where our vocation to make things more straight will be heard or missed.

But what is our point of departure? Our text startles us again:

> A voice says, "Cry!"
>   And I said, "What shall I cry?"
> All flesh is grass,
>   and all its beauty is like the flower of the field.
> The grass withers, the flower fades
>   when the breath of the LORD blows upon it;
>   surely the people is grass.
> The grass withers, the flower fades,
>   but the word of our God will stand forever.

We cannot dismiss this as small town theology of rustics who live close to the margin of existence and who therefore are especially sensitive to the tenuousness of life. No, this comes from urban and urbane Babylon, with its avenues and markets, its culture and prosperity. Perhaps those Judeans were as impressed by that advanced technological society as are certain Protestant theologians today, those of us who came up in small town, pietistic churches and who now find that we can enjoy Jack Daniels as we consort with the estahlishnent, and cannot get over the wonder of it all. But whatever may have been the situation, our prophet starts with the insight that *all* flesh, not just Babylonian flesh, is grass. He does not say what the author of Ecclesiastes says—that nothing is really worthwhile because everything is vanity. Rather, it has no permanence; nor should we cheapen the insight by restricting it to the problem of longevity. All that man is and does is grass. Shall we be specific where it counts? Scholarship is grass, for the books that are "in" today are passé tomorrow; curriculum revision is grass, for what is avant garde today is rear gaard tomorrow. Leading theologies are grass, green with promise today and brown with death tomorrow. One after another the brave new models of today are the Edsels of tomorrow. Even those who trade on this sort of thing implicitly admit it; why else would we have a paperback series, *New Theology* No. 1, No. 2, No. 3, and No. 4?

Now we must not be confused by the salvo which this prophet fires across our bow. We are prone to say, "Well, if all flesh is grass, why labor to make anything straight? If all flesh is grass, what difference does it make?" The reason we jump to this conclusion is that we think he is stating the *basis* for our vocation, outlining its ground. But this is not the case at all. Rather, he is setting the horizons against which we labor, warning us in advance not to take ourselves too seriously. Moreover, when the momentariness of all our striving is clear we can perceive that we are not and *cannot be* the basis for work or the ground of our hope. Rather, our hope and labor are derived from that which stands over against the frailty of man's work.

The central section of the chapter now moves to announce the character of God, to suggest something about the glory that is not yet manifest, whose ways are not our ways, who is not the cosmic analog to our noblest works or the logarithmic function of our interaction. True, we have difficulty with the way he goes about speaking of the Majestic One, for he points to the magnitude and splendor of the cosmos. We have no patience with any form of the cosmological argument for the existence of God, and with good reason; ever since Hume these arguments have lost their power to compel belief in God. That is why we said at the outset that we cannot argue our way into hope. Yet, our poet-prophet is not interesting in establishing the logical necessity of believing in God, and we miss the point if we read him as if he were. Rather, the world around him and above him induces him to wonder, and from wonder he moves to reflection, and from reElection to articulation. So he says, in effect, "What do you think the word 'God' means? Do you think that the mightiest powers—the stars, with which Babylonians were especially concerned—rule over him? No, he rules over them, and when he calls the roll none is absent and none shows up late." This God is not to be understood as an object chosen by men as worthy of their worship; rather, men are chosen by him to be worthy of his service. Yet this is so hard to take in and to live by.

The reason is disclosed in the closing strophe. The hearers think God has either abandoned them or cannot make good his word. They think their situation is too much for God. Because they have no hope they think he has no future.

> Why do you say, O Jacob,
> and speak, O Israel,
> "My way is hid from the LORD,
> and my right is disregarded by my God?"

Do not these lines expose the basis for our non-hope, for our lack of direction and vocation? Are we not tempted to say that Isaiah's way, or Paul's way, or Augustine's or Luther's was not hid from the Lord God because after all they were prophets, apostles and saints, but that surely our case is different? But what kind of inverted pride is it that maintains that our situation is beyond God's ken, and outside the range of his grace and power? Cannot he who brought back Israel out of Egypt, Babylon, and Auschwitz, who set before this people the high calling of being a light to the nations call us to our task in our time and place? Is ours the first geneaion of Christians to find itself without compass or goal? Are the church and seminary in our time the first to need their vision restored and their vocation renewed? What else does the history of Israel and that of the church show us but just this—that time and again the vision must be seen afresh and the vocation be appropriated anew! Neither our text nor the history of God's people will let us say that our way is hid from God, that he cannot reach us or redeem us from what we now are for what we must be.

But our text does more thaa expose us. It offers a redeeming word. It does not argue but makes a promise concerning God's integrity, his faithfulness to himself and to his people.

> Have you not known?
> Have you not heard? . . .

> He does not faint or grow weary,
>> and his understanding is unsearchable.
> He gives power to the faint,
>> and to him who has not might he increases strength.
> Even youths shall faint and be weary,
>> and young men shall fall exhausted;
> but they who wait for the Lord shall renew their strength,
>> they shall mount up with wings like eagles,
> they shall run and not be weary,
>> they shall walk and not faint.

Who receives this power, and who finds strength in the wilderness? They who wait for the Lord. And with this word the prophet startles us again, we who cannot wait for anyone or anything. I know this is a dangerous text because to those wanting "Freedom Now!" Whigs and Tories will always make it say, "Do nothing, just wait for the Lord." Yet our text does not speak about impatience in the quest for justice. Indeed, how would what is crooked ever be made straight if we were to squat beside the job and wait for God to act? No, our text has something else in mind. It speaks of our impatience with God, of our demand for epiphany now, of our insistence that the glory of the Lord reveal itself so unambiguously now that we no longer need to walk and work by faith alone but can march by sight instead. But the prophet promises strength in this wilderness, this history, this grass—strength to those who know how to labor as they wait because they know for whom they wait. To hear that the Eternal gives strength is to hear the promise and to have hope renewed, and this is to discover that strength is here.

But you say, "This is Advent, the time for celebrating the coming of God's man. Is not ours the situation of fulfilment rather than of hope? Does not the gospel announce that God has kept his Word, has fulfilled his promise and brought salvation?" This is indeed the good tidings which we celebrate at Advent. But why do we still talk about hope? Why do we not simply celebrate the consummation and the fulfilment?

That obstreperous apostle, Paul, put his finger on it when he insisted that we are saved for hope. More than any other New Testament writer he exposed the fact that we stand between salvation begun and salvation not yet consummated, between already and not yet, that faith itself is confidence that what God has begun he will see through. God's man Jesus does not save us from the life of hope but confirms it. The advent of Jesus does not put Isaiah out of commisiion, or retire his text to the museum where we can observe with pride the state of man that we have transcended. No, his coming is a renewed pledge that God does not grow weary, that our way is not hid from the Lord, that making things right is not beyond the range of his capacity. That Jesus is the fulfilment of Israel's hope and vocation does not mean we have nothing more to learn from the Old Testament, that it no longer discloses who we are. Rather, to say that Jesus is the Messiah means precisely tfat this text is now our own, that the God of whom it speaks is our God, that the hope it nourishes is our hope, that the glory of the Lord which we have glimpsed in Messiah Jesus will indeed be seen by all flesh. Who can be grasped by what Jesus is all about and not be moved to hope? Whose life can be touched by the presence of God's Spirit and not be moved to yearn for the consummation of what is now tasted, a consummation that includes all mankind. Or are we called to be Corinthians, whom Paul taunts, "Already you are sated!" No, we are among those who hunger and thirst for righteousness, for rectitude, and do so because we have tasted what this is like and are confident that we and all mankind will he satisfied. And so we lean into the future, God's future pledged anew and made certain in the advent of Jesus.

Besides, we do not celebrate his Advent unless we follow in his wake, and share his life and mission. Nothing in the Gospels suggests that his mission was to organize a community like that at the Dead Sea which thought that by disciplined study alone would the Lord's way be readied. No, when he chose disciples he taught them and sent them out to do as he did, to preach good news to the poor, expel the demonic and to exemplify in advance what the coming of the Lord was all about. Who can stand in his wake and there celebrate Advent and not have his vocation renewed and his hope rekindled? Who can pledge his own life to the life of God's man and not move into the future expecting that what God inaugurated will yet come to pass? The hope we celebrate is not the judicious inference from so-called Christian civilization or church history. Rather, it is grounded in the integrity of God, and in the firm expectation that God will make good what Jesus was all about.

This is the God whose promise calls us so to live and so to labor that we make straight in this desert a highway for our God, and to do so because he has implanted within us the vision of his glory which for a moment broke through in Jesus. They who see in him what God's coming means are they who, even in the wilderness, shall run and not be weary.

www.ingramcontent.com/pod-product-compliance
Lightning Source LLC
Chambersburg PA
CBHW031432150426
43191CB00006B/483